Pagan Portals
Kitchen Witchcraft

WHAT PEOPLE ARE SAYING ABOUT

KITCHEN WITCHCRAFT

I like this ... it's light, friendly and good fun to read. One important facet of traditional Craft is the use of the kitchen and everyday implements to create magical goodies. I like the way the author brings the reader into the kitchen and makes the whole thing inclusive like having a cosy chat over the cauldron. A great addition to the Pagan Portals series.
Mélusine Draco, author of numerous popular books

Rachel Patterson's *Kitchen Witchcraft* is an excellent introduction to witchcraft's system of correspondences, and reminds us that the ingredients of nature's magic surround us whether we live in an Old World witch's cottage or a modern high rise.
Mark Carter, author of *Stalking the Goddess*

A wonderful little book which will get anyone started on Kitchen Witchery. Informative, and easy to follow.
Janet Farrar & Gavin Bone, authors *A Witches Bible, Witches Goddess and Inner Mysteries*

I am very proud to write this endorsement for Rachel's book, *Kitchen Witchcraft*. Rachel is very sensible and down to earth, both qualities that are rare nowadays, but which I really admire. Kitchen Witchcraft is becoming increasingly possible as people try and merge spiritual and everyday life. Rachel's book contains plenty of great suggestions for kitchen witchery and I particularly like her emphasis on learning to love what you have, yet learning to adapt and grow too, which is an essential part of the Craft.

The beauty of this book is the ease with which Rachel blends the magical with the everyday, something I consider to be the true essence of all witchcraft. Her writing is a friendly, personal account that immediately invites us to feel we are there in the kitchen with her. This is particularly helpful for those who work as solitaries.

Kitchen Witchcraft contains plenty of ideas about the seasons, elements, festivals, gardens, working with candles and crystals and – best of all in my view – recipes for potions and incense etc. These will make even the newest beginner feel very 'witchy' indeed!

Tylluan Penry, author of *Seeking the Green, Magic on the Breath, Magical Properties of Plants, Staying on the Old Track* and *the Essential Guide to Psychic Self Defence*

It's a great little book, it's packed with all kinds of information any Pagan would find very useful from candle magic and cleaning fluids to details of the elements. This is something you need to keep handy in your kitchen for helping you with your spells, your incense and your day to day magical life.

Siusaidh Ceanadach, author of *A Ceremony for Every Occasion* & *Let's Talk About Pagan Festivals*

Pagan Portals
Kitchen Witchcraft

Rachel Patterson

Winchester, UK
Washington, USA

First published by Moon Books, 2013
Moon Books is an imprint of John Hunt Publishing Ltd., Laurel House, Station Approach,
Alresford, Hants, SO24 9JH, UK
office1@jhpbooks.net
www.johnhuntpublishing.com
www.moon-books.net

For distributor details and how to order please visit the 'Ordering' section on our website.

Text copyright: Rachel Patterson 2012

ISBN: 978 1 78099 843 5

A CIP catalogue record for this book is available from the British Library.

Design: Stuart Davies

Printed and bound by CPI Group (UK) Ltd, Croydon, CR0 4YY

We operate a distinctive and ethical publishing philosophy in all
areas of our business, from our global network of authors to
production and worldwide distribution.

CONTENTS

Who Am I?

My craft name is Tansy Firedragon and I have been a witch for many years now, originally studying on my own as a solitary from books and the internet. I then spent a year and a half studying and gaining a Wiccan first degree with an online school. Then I joined another online school for seven years. During that time I worked through the first, second and third Wiccan degrees. I studied with Janet Farrar and Gavin Bone on their Progressive Magick course, passing with a distinction. I have also taken courses on druidry, tarot, pendulums, herbalism, empathy, witches runes and aromatherapy. I have Reiki Level I & II attunement. In 2011 I was made High Priestess and in 2012 ordained as a Minister of the Universal Life Church.

I am a member of the Dorset Grove Druids, as well as being High Priestess in my own coven co-run by my lovely sisters in the craft, The Kitchen Witch Coven of Natural Witchery, which allows me to attend lots of outside rituals in wonderful sacred places within the UK.

I am co-founder and a leadership team member of the online Kitchen Witch School of Natural Witchcraft. We also have a facebook page and a blog.

www.kitchenwitchhearth.com

www.kitchenwitchuk.blogspot.co.uk

www.facebook.com/kitchenwitchuk

I have a personal blog www.tansyfiredragon.blogspot.co.uk and facebook page www.facebook.com/racheltansypatterson

Email: tansyfiredragon@yahoo.com

My craft is a combination of old religion witchcraft, wicca, kitchen witchery, green witchery and hoodoo. My heart is that of a Kitchen Witch. I am blessed with a wonderful husband, lovely children, a fabulous family and good friends.

Introduction

A woman stands hunched over an old wooden table, pestle and mortar in her hands, grinding away at a mixture of ingredients. A large white candle stands on the table beside her, the flame flickering and spluttering. Open in front of her lies a huge leather bound book, the pages well worn and filled with beautifully written spells. Sounds like a scene from medieval times? Actually it could be now; it could be me (or you) in a town house kitchen, or an apartment in the city.

This is a witch at work, same scene, same utensils, and same ingredients now as centuries ago.

A witch works with nature, in tune with the earth, working and living along with the ebb and flow of the seasons. Spring is for cleaning, clearing out clutter, sweeping out the cobwebs and setting new goals. Summer is a time for celebrating the Sun God, for basking in his glow, working on projects, gardening and creating. Autumn is a time to be thankful for the harvest, to give thanks for all that we have and to start storing away for the winter. Winter itself is for reflection, a time to pull up a chair by the fire and think back over what you have achieved. All of these things can be done physically, mentally and spiritually with each turn of the Wheel of the Year.

As a witch you can have all the right equipment – wands, athames, pentagrams etc, but you will find a Kitchen Witch tends to prefer to use what is to hand. A finger serves purpose as a wand, a feather for the element of Air, a pebble for the element of earth... you get the drift.

A Kitchen Witch will create... recipes, crafts, lotions and potions. When a friend is poorly a Kitchen Witch will work a spell to aid, but will also make some homemade soup, putting healing energy into making it, adding healing energy with each vegetable and herb that is added.

To connect with the divine a witch will step outside, take a cup of coffee and sit in the garden, to be outside with nature… that is where the connection is. Feel the wind in your hair, the sun on your face, feel the grass beneath your feet, the free and wild feeling of being at one with nature, Mother Earth and her bounty.

A Kitchen Witch will also get that connection in the kitchen, working with herbs, spices, plants and produce. Everything a Kitchen Witch makes is made with love, affection and a little bit of magic.

Here I have shared with you just some of the ways of the witch and the craft, hoping that together we can seek out the Kitchen Witch within.

Kitchen Cupboards and Tools

This is not all that is in my cupboards, but it is a basic list of everyday items to start with.

Salt
Chilli powder
Cinnamon
Paprika
Cloves
Nutmeg
Parsley
Sage
Thyme
Rosemary
Marjoram
Washed, dried and crushed egg shells
Lavender buds
Rose petals

Creating a Sacred Kitchen

So you might see the kitchen as a wonderful creative space, you might loathe it completely and only ever use the microwave. But it is still a kitchen; it is still a space that you have to make food in. So how about making it a magical space?

In my ideal world I would have a huge farmhouse kitchen with a large wooden kitchen table in the centre for everyone to sit round, the table bleached from being scrubbed over so many years, herbs hanging overhead drying and a huge oven range to cook on... yeah right... I live in a terraced house in the city! OK so it's a nice 1920's terraced house with real fireplaces, but the kitchen is never going to fit a farmhouse table. So you make the most of what you have.

So let's imagine that stepping into your kitchen, whether you will only be in there for the six minutes it takes for the microwave to ping or whether you will be in there for a couple of hours baking your own cakes... that it makes you feel magical, that it makes you feel as if you have stepped into a place of power. Well, we can create that.

It doesn't have to take lots of time or money, you don't have to take on board all the ideas given, but it will give you some suggestions.

Make it Yours

Go take a look in your kitchen, yep go on... I will wait...

What do you see? Do you love the decoration? Do you love the colour? Does it look like something from a country kitchen or does it look like something from the local science lab? You need to think of your kitchen as yours, it ought to reflect you and your connection to the divine. Yes I know we need it to be practical too, but you can 'make it yours'.

Put a pretty rug on the floor (one that can be chucked in the washing machine).

Paint spirals, Goddess symbols, flowers, leaves – whatever takes your fancy – on the cupboard doors or use stencils.

Check out the stores at Samhain, they usually stock lots of interesting bits and pieces that can be used to decorate a witch's kitchen.

Hang up pictures or items from nature on the walls.

Go mad, go wild, go funky (my own kitchen has lots of witches on broomsticks hanging from the ceiling, witch balls too, lots of witch figures on shelves and a besom hanging on one wall, although you don't have to be quite that mad).

Make like Snow White...

Yep, I mean cleaning; yes I know it's boring. And I don't expect us all to spend hours every day making it clinical, but if the kitchen smells yucky because it's dirty and if you can't actually see the work surfaces because of clutter you aren't going to feel calm and connected in there.

But you can make the cleaning magical and spiritual.

Sing as you clean, something pagan that brings the Goddess into the kitchen as you sweep and mop. If you don't know any particular songs just make something up – singing will help the work get done faster too.

I also think that being bare foot helps to connect when you are at home too, not just in the kitchen but all over the house.

Wear a specific apron, I have one that has witchcraft symbols all over it; you could make your own. Keep it as your magical apron, the one that when you put it on turns you into Super Kitchen Witch ;-)

What about cleaning products? Now there are some very good eco-friendly cleaning products on the market, but we haven't all got the endless budget to pay for them, so if you haven't, how about having a go at making your own?

Make a compost bin, use all your fruit and vegetable scraps, and shredded paper, to make your own compost.

Recycle. I am lucky enough to have a recycle collection scheme; they collect paper, plastic and card once a fortnight.

Ju ju your floor wash – make a good strong cup of herbal tea, strain it and add the liquid to your floor wash, it not only makes it smell nice, but if you use herbs that have cleansing and purifying properties you add magic to your wash too. You can even use herbal tea bags.

Once you have done with the actual physical cleaning give the kitchen a smudge with some sage, lavender or rosemary or even an incense stick will do. Waft the smoke into every corner, even into the cupboards.

Once you have finished, stop and look around again, this is your place of being, it is a sacred place now, one that is ready to make magic in. Send out your energy into your kitchen... own it.

Make Friends with the Appliances

Ok so I am not suggesting you give the cooker a name and hold regular conversations with it – unless you want to... But there are usually a lot of electrical appliances in your kitchen and they all rely on energy to work. Being afraid of using those appliances can send out negative vibes and they might be unhappy to co-operate when we need them too. Consider your appliances your allies; they are your household pixies.

A Kitchen Altar

I think having an altar in your kitchen gives it a focal point; it doesn't have to be big. I have a small green man shelf and on top of that I have a tiny vase (it is actually a small candle holder) that I put a fresh flower in regularly, and it has representations of the elements – a shell, a feather, a red crystal and a pebble. The top of the shelf surface is no bigger than the palm of my hand. You could just have a Goddess statue on a shelf or even just a Goddess picture hung on the wall. Your kitchen altar is where you honour deity as a Kitchen Goddess. You might like to actually choose a particular Goddess to have as your kitchen deity, one that is connected to home and hearth, or you might just want to keep it general – it is your kitchen, your choice. You might even prefer to have a kitchen faerie or a kitchen dragon instead.

You could use candles, these are representations of the element of Fire, which is very prominent in a kitchen, and it also represents the home and hearth. It could even just be a small tea light. You could light the candle when you begin the food preparation, use it as your way to honour deity, light it and ask them to bless the food you are about to prepare.

Leave an offering on your kitchen altar for each meal you prepare (just remember to leave something not too sticky, and remove it the following day).

Have fun with your altar design, use natural objects, and decorate it for the seasons with an acorn, leaves or flowers. If you have the space you could even go to town on it and decorate it with kitchen items – cutlery, tiny pots or pans from dolls house furniture.

Whatever you end up creating for your altar and however big or small it is, use it as a focal point in your kitchen. Just take a moment before you start to prepare a meal by standing in front of the altar and asking for a blessing.

Cooking up some Magic

OK, so you don your 'Kitchen Witch' apron, your kitchen is all tidy, and your altar is all pretty. Then what?

Even the most domesticated goddess won't feel like cooking every single day, so just give yourself a few moments before you start to get yourself in the right frame of mind, stand in front of your altar or your Goddess picture/statue and calm, centre and ground yourself.

If you are making a meal for yourself or to share you don't want to be doing it whilst sending out negative energies. Part of the cooking process allows you to 'add' magic to the meal, whether it is in the form of herbs, ingredients or just the positive energy you use whilst you cook. Even if the only cooking you do is to open the packet and warm it up.

Whilst you are preparing your meal try to think and feel positive, whilst you are stirring the pots try to stir them deosil (clockwise) to bring good energies in. As you add ingredients really take notice of their colour, their shape, their energy, the connection they had with the earth.

And, of course, you can tailor your ingredients for the meal you are making. If you are making a romantic meal for a loved one you could add items that have love as one of their magical properties such as cloves or basil or make a pie from apples – charging the ingredients with your intent. If you are making a dish for the family you could add cinnamon as this brings the magical properties of a happy home, safety and protection. I have listed here some of the more common herbs and foods with their magical properties, there are more detailed lists on the net, but go with your instincts too.

You know the archetypes, like asparagus and oysters being aphrodisiacs, but there are many other foods that have magical properties such as:

Black pepper – stimulating
Cabbage – luck
Carrots – healing
Cashew – money
Celery – mental powers, lust, psychic powers
Chilli pepper – hex breaking, love
Chocolate – comforting
Coriander – stimulating
Corn/maize – protection, luck
Cucumber – chastity, healing, fertility
Grape – fertility, mental powers, money

Onion – strengthening and purifying
Leek – love, protection, exorcism
Lemon – longevity, purification, love, friendship
Lettuce – chastity, protection, love, sleep
Lime – healing, love, protection
Olive – healing, peace, fertility, protection, lust
Onions – protection, exorcism, healing, money, prophetic
   dreams, lust
Orange – love, luck, money
Pea – money, love
Peach – love, exorcism, longevity, fertility, wishes
Pear – lust, love
Pecan – money, employment
Pepper, black – protection, exorcism
Pineapple – luck, money, chastity
Pomegranate – luck, wishes, wealth, fertility
Potato – good for rheumatism
Rice – protection, rain, money, fertility
Spinach – mental and physical stimulant
Strawberry – love, luck
Sugar – love, lust
Tea (black) – riches, courage, strength
Tomato – prosperity, protection, love
Walnut – health, mental powers, infertility, wishes
Wheat – fertility, money

And herbs:

Allspice – money, luck, healing
Anise – protection, purification, youth
Balm, lemon – love, success, healing
Basil – love, wealth, protection
Bay – protection, psychic powers, healing, purification,
   strength

Cardamom – lust, love

Chamomile – money, sleep, love, protection, calming, sleep

Cinnamon – spirituality, success, healing, power, psychic powers, lust, protection, love

Clove – protection, love, money

Coriander – love, health, healing

Dill – protection, money, lust, love

Fennel – protection, healing, purification

Fenugreek – money

Garlic – protection, healing, lust

Ginger – love, money, success, power

Juniper – protection, love, exorcism, health

Lavender – love, protection, sleep, chastity, purification, happiness, peace

Marjoram – protection, love, happiness, health, money

Mint – money, lust, healing, exorcism, protection

Nettle – exorcism, protection, healing, lust

Nutmeg – luck, money, health, fidelity

Parsley – lust, protection, purification

Rosemary – protection, love, lust, mental powers, exorcism, purification, healing, sleep, youth

Sage – immortality, longevity, wisdom, protection, wishes

Thyme – health, healing, sleep, psychic powers, love, purification, courage

Turmeric – purification

Vanilla – love, lust, mental powers

Cooking with the Wheel of the Year

I think working with the seasons in your kitchen is very important. For a start, fruit and vegetables taste better when they are in season as they have been allowed to grow naturally at the proper time of the year and haven't been forced. Organic vegetables are obviously best if you can use them because again they taste better and they are seasonal, but I do appreciate that we can't always afford them. We have an organic vegetable box scheme where I live and, although the price is comparable with the organic vegetables in the supermarket, they are still more expensive than non organic so I have a box delivered every other week. It's like a lovely surprise every fortnight as I don't know what will be in the box. I try to buy locally when I can too; it's not so easy in the city, but do have a look in your locality for farm shops or farmers' markets.

Not only do you get the better tasting produce when you eat seasonally, I think it helps connect you with the turning of the Wheel too. Fresh sweet strawberries in the summer months make you think and feel of warm summer days, pumpkins and squashes make you think of fallen leaves and dark evenings. It all helps to keep you in touch, to keep that connection to the earth and her cycles. It will also help you to keep track of the Sabbats and understand them more fully. You don't have to prepare a grand feast for each one, but have a think at least about what food our ancestors would have eaten when they celebrated.

And, of course, there are breads and cakes that you could make specifically for Sabbats and Esbats, crescent-shape cookies are fantastic for moon celebrations.

If you harvest a lot of herbs that you won't use all at once, if you dry them for magical uses you can also freeze them, make herbal tea blends; make herb jellies, vinegars and oils with them too.

Witchy Workings in the Kitchen

You can work some spells in the kitchen using the items you have and the produce you use, here are some ideas:

To release pent up emotions – this one has got to be so simple... chop onions. Let the emotions flow as your tears flow from the onions.

Release of anger – chop, chop like you have never chopped before. But please be careful of your fingers. Tenderising meat is good for this too, but be careful not to beat it too much!

Releasing old habits – peel those root vegetables, as you take off the old skin release your old habits, as you see the fresh, clean surface underneath visualize a refreshed you.

To boost your energy – shake it baby. Make a salad dressing in a jar and shake it, dance round the kitchen with it.

To bring peace and calm – make something that requires looking after and stirring, such as risotto or a custard, feel yourself becoming calmer and more peaceful with each turn of the spoon.

To ground – well this one should be obvious – grab yourself a potato or a parsnip, something that has grown in the soil. Hold onto it and connect with its earth energies.

Bringing things together – to gain balance – try blending or whisking, mixing up batter, something that involves bringing different ingredients together to make a whole.

When Inspiration Escapes

Even though I love to cook some days I just don't feel inspired, it is these days that I sometimes cave in and order takeaway and that's OK, we all need a day off and a treat now and then. On other days when inspiration has departed and I don't have the funds for takeaway I get out my cook books and look for inspiration or watch a food channel on TV. Or if you have the time, go out and have a wander around your local farm shop or farmers' market; be inspired by the produce itself.

You might also find that what you feel like cooking will change depending on where your body is in its cycle, where the moon is in her phase or how you are feeling – keep an eye on it and see if you can note any patterns.

It's Not all about Food

What? I hear you cry... surely it's always about food? Ha! nope. Your witchy kitchen is also a good place to make lotions and potions. You can make lots of lovely body lotions in your kitchen too, along with bath salts, balms and incense. You could also make your own perfume blends, herbal sachets, pressed flowers, smudge sticks and medicine bags.

What Does a Kitchen Witch use for Magical Tools?

Cauldron – a casserole dish or Dutch oven. Make sure it is an old one or one you don't mind being spoilt because as you burn things in it, it will remove any non-stick surface.

Wand – I have made wands myself from sticks and twigs. You can also use your finger or a wooden spoon works very well too.

Athame – a kitchen knife or even a potato peeler.

Chalice – a pretty glass or cup – sometimes you can find really nice pieces in the charity shops/thrift stores.

Candlesticks – I have two very pretty silver candlesticks to hold my Goddess and God candles, I purchased them for a few pence in a charity shop.

Pentacle – this can be made from all sorts of natural items – sticks and twigs bound together with hemp string look really effective. Or you could draw a pentagram on a round flat pebble from the beach. If you are any good with a needle you could make a cross stitch or embroidered one.

Offering dish – I have a couple of dishes that I put crystals or herbs in when I am making a request to deity or thanking them. One I made myself, which is very basic, I formed from air drying clay (it was only a few pence from a local craft store) and the other is just a large round flat shell I found on the beach.

Elements – to represent the elements you can use a pebble or a dish of soil or salt for Earth, a feather or incense for Air, a candle for Fire or I sometimes use a red coloured crystal, and for Water a small dish of water or a shell works perfectly.

Celebrating the Sabbats

We celebrate the Sabbats to mark the turning of the Wheel of the Year to walk the path our ancestors followed in honouring the Earth and the seasons.

Yule

Yule is a time of rebirth, when the sun stops retreating and stands still (which is the meaning of the word solstice) then begins to return.

This is a time to dance, sing and feast. Make a Yule log, hang mistletoe, drink wassail, light candles, decorate your Yule tree and celebrate the blessings of having family and friends.

It is also the time when the Holly King, who represents winter, fights with the Oak King, who represents summer. They battle and the Holly King is defeated, the Oak King stands to reign until the Summer Solstice.

I don't necessarily like the cold, but I do love the festive season, always have done ever since I was a child. My parents made a huge effort at this time of the year and still do and I have followed on in the tradition.

To me Yule is a magical time, it is all about family and friends. It is celebrating what we have and who we have to share it with. The nights are dark, but we have warm homes to stay inside and keep us protected. We have loving family and friends to share our time with, and whilst I am not a big lover of snow from the practical point of view it does look so beautiful when it is first laid, so white and pure and untouched, very magical indeed.

I have two large Yule trees, one in the dining room that is decorated with reds and golds, plus lots of natural decorations as well. Then I have a tree in the lounge too that is all decorated with greens and golds and our bauble collection. Each year that my husband and I have celebrated a Yule together we have purchased a special tree bauble, they are all shapes and sizes and sometimes represent something from that year. And once our children came along, they have had a bauble for each Yule they have celebrate. They get to choose it.

My main altar will be decorated with red and gold and sparkly faerie lights, my working altar will also be red and gold. Lots of candles and lots of glitter. I also have fake flowers – mistletoe, ivy, holly and pine cones – that I use as well.

I also make an extra effort over the winter months to make sure there is plenty of food out in the garden for the birds.

Foods for Yule – nuts, apples, cider, pork, dried fruit, cookies, mulled wine.

Colours for this celebration are red, green, white, gold and silver.

Make incense using cedar, ginger, cinnamon, pine, rosemary, frankincense, myrrh, nutmeg and cloves.

Decorate with candles, evergreens, holly, mistletoe, lights, Yule log, wreaths and bells.

Imbolc

Imbolc is when the first signs of spring growth are seen. Underneath the Earth new life is stirring.

This festival is sacred to the Goddess Brighid, the Goddess of healing, poetry and fire. She breathes life into the Earth wiping away the darkness of the winter. This festival honours the Goddess in her Maiden form as she waits for the return of the sun. It is a time for new beginnings and renewal.

For me after Yule there is a bit of a dip, a bit of a lull. January for me is a quiet, non event kind of a month. The festivities are over, probably in the days of our ancestors food stores were beginning to run low, the weather is always cold, snowy or wet and no one has any money. But it is also the start of the new calendar year, full of possibilities and promises. A time to stay inside and take stock and plan all the wonderful things to do for the coming year. And as Imbolc comes upon us hopefully there are a few odd signs the spring is on its way. Imbolc is all about the returning light, the days are ever so slowly getting longer, the dark nights getting ever so slowly shorter.

My altar will be decorated a white cloth, I will have lots of white, pale green and pale yellow candles and will put some greenery from the garden in a vase. I have a couple of variegated evergreen shrubs in the garden so the white and green go very well with Imbolc.

Foods for Imbolc – spicy dishes, dairy, seeds, herbal teas, garlic and onions.

Colours for this celebration are pale blue, pale pink, white, yellow and pale green.

Make incense using basil, bay, chamomile, cinnamon, sage, frankincense, myrrh, sandalwood, vanilla and violet.

Decorate with candles, lights, besoms, flowers, Brighid's crosses, horseshoes, seeds and seasonal flowers.

Ostara

Ostara is a festival of fertility of the land and marks the time when day and night are equal in length. It is a time for new beginnings, fertility, wishes, rebirth, renewal, bringing your desires into your life.

The God and the Goddess are courting at this time, so it is a good time to focus on the balance between male and female energies within ourselves.

And it's all about the chocolate ;-) Spring is bursting out all over as they say. Ostara is fresh, it is the earth waking up and starting to show the signs of life, plants and animals beginning the journey towards the summer months. It is fertility in an eggshell, literally. The egg symbolises new life, new hope and the promise of expectation. It is a time to start new projects, to begin a new phase of your life.

My altar will be decorated with white or yellow cloth, and

then covered with tiny fluffy chicks and lambs (not real ones obviously…) I also have some beautiful tiny painted china eggs that I hang on my main altar. Hopefully the camellia will be flowering in my garden too and I like to float some of the flowers from that in a small dish of water on the altar too.

Foods for Ostara – eggs, edible flowers, fish, sweet breads, chocolate, honey cake, dairy, nuts and seasonal fruit.

Colours for this celebration are pale green, bright green, pale blue, pale yellow, pale pink and white.

Make incense with violet, ginger, broom, sage, lavender, rose and strawberry.

Decorate with coloured eggs, butterflies, spring flowers, lambs, rabbits, hares and chicks.

Beltane

Beltane is a time when we celebrate fertility, with the sacred marriage of the God and Goddess. This is all about celebrating life! It is the Earth awakening from her sleep and putting forth new growth. Flowers and plants are all starting to bloom and summer is not too far away. Traditionally it is time for the Bel fire, lit from the nine sacred woods – birch, oak, rowan, willow, hawthorn, hazel, apple, grapevine and fir. The fire is healing and purifying and symbolises the burning away of winter and the fruitfulness of summer.

Beltane is all about sex basically. It is the union of the God and the Goddess. In ancient pagan times it was the festival where men and women got together literally to celebrate.

It is May Day, it is the maypole which is basically ahem… male… and danced around by nubile young virgins hoping for that special man to whisk them away. The maypole is quite often red and white striped – the red symbolising the female the white symbolising the male.

My altar will be decorated with a red cloth with red and white candles. By this time there will hopefully be some early roses in the garden to put in a vase.

This is the time of the year when plans you put into action should be starting to happen, if they aren't it is time to sort them out and set them in the right direction.

It is also usually the time when my chimenea gets its first use of the year, I do love to burn my spells! Beltane is also a fire festival, so I like to work with the element of Fire to complement the Sabbat.

Foods for Beltane – dairy, sweets, custards, ice cream, honey, salads, fruit punch, oat cakes and fruits.

Colours for this celebration are red and white to represent the God and the Goddess, dark green, blue, pastel colours and yellow.

Make incense with frankincense, lilac, rose, vanilla, honey-suckle, lavender, patchouli, meadowsweet and sandalwood.

Decorate with maypoles, baskets of flowers, eggs, chalices and candles to represent fire.

Litha

Litha is the peak of the seasonal cycle, when the hours of daylight are longest. It is a time to soak up the sun, to celebrate the end of the waxing year and to welcome in the waning year. It is also a fertility festival. This is also one of the Sabbats where the veil between our world and that of the Faerie is thin, so we also welcome them.

Summer should be warm hazy days, fields of long grass, butterflies flittering in and out, bees buzzing, but in the UK we can't always guarantee that.

However, Litha is when the sun is at its highest, the longest day of sunlight and the shortest night. Then it is the slippery slope heading towards the darker half of the year.

The Holly King and the Oak King fight again at this point, the Holly King winning this time to rule the dark half of the year.

It seems quite a bitter sweet celebration really, we celebrate the Sun King in all his glory, we thank him for sending the light and the warm to grow the crops and the food, but then we are also saying farewell to him too.

Not long after Litha are the school holidays so I spend a lot more time outside than I do in the school term, trying to prise my children from the computer to play outside. I also spend a lot of time in the garden during the spring and summer months. I like to go out first thing in the morning and say hello to the world and put bread out for the birds, I then go out again in the evenings to water all the plants and potter about dead heading withered flowers and tidying up. I also like to eat my lunch in the garden if I can too; it is my quiet time, the time to connect with nature and be at one.

My altar will be decorated with a yellow and gold cloth, yellow candles and fresh flowers from the garden.

Foods for Litha are honey, vegetables and fruit, bread, ale and mead.

Colours for this celebration are white, red, yellow, green and blue.

Make incense with chamomile, copal, fennel, lavender, lemon, oak, pine, sandalwood, thyme and ylang ylang.

Decorate with symbols of the sun, sunflowers, oak leaves, fresh flowers, fruit, seashells and images of Faerie.

Lughnasadgh

Lughnasadgh is the first harvest; we celebrate abundance and prosperity. The sun is losing its power; although not gone yet he wanes. A time of reaping what we have sown, not only from the harvest point of view, but also personally.

My working altar will be decorated with yellow and gold material, it will have gold and yellow candles and a vase with fresh flowers in. I will make a salt dough wreath with flowers and leaves on it that I hang above my altar. Living in the centre of the city it is difficult to connect with the essence of the harvest, but on our trips out we pass fields full of grain. In my own small garden I harvest herbs regularly and collect seed heads from those plants that flower early. The herbs I dry on trays in the conservatory. I also get together with family, where we sit and drink, eat and talk, I would imagine after the harvest our ancestors would have sat back even if only for a short while and feasted and made toasts to the harvest.

Also called Lammas, this is the Christian word meaning 'loaf mass' when newly baked loaves are placed on the altar.

Foods for Litha – bread, nuts, crab apples, rice, lamb, wine, ale, cider, herbal tea, grains, berries and vegetables.

Colours for this celebration are yellow, gold, orange, green, brown.

Make incense with rose, rosemary, chamomile, sandalwood, heather, clover, basil, mint and woods.

Decorate with corn, cornucopias, sheaves of grain, vegetables and fruit, corn dollies, bread, a sickle and fresh flowers.

Mabon

Mabon is the last harvest. It is also the Autumn Equinox when day and night are equal. A time to give thanks to the sunlight and prepare for the winter months ahead. Honour your ancestors, finish up projects and make ready for the darker, colder months to follow.

To me Mabon is the beginning of autumn; it is when the weather starts to change. The mornings become crisp and fresh, there is that slight chill in the air. The leaves are starting to tinge their way to autumn colours. The last of the harvest is being brought in and people and animals are starting to make preparations for the coming winter months. You still get warm days though and we make the most of them. I spend time in the garden tidying up and clearing away the end of the summer bedding plants, cutting back the clematis and the roses. It is a time to celebrate the abundance that nature has provided over the warmer months. It is apple time! Apples seem to represent Mabon perfectly. They have spent the summer months growing and are picked in the autumn, some to be eaten straight away, others to be stored to last through the darker winter months. And if you cut an apple through the centre you see the pentagram, the sign of the witch and for me Mabon heralds the beginning of the Season of the Witch! The darker months when we spend a lot more time indoors, in front of the fire, reading, cooking, eating, spending time with family and cooking up ideas, spells and schemes!

My altar will be decorated with orange, red and yellow cloth, the candles will also be of the same colour. I will put out apples and the last of the flowers from the garden. I will also put some nuts on it too.

Foods for Mabon – bread, nuts, apples, root vegetables, squashes and pomegranates.

Colours for this celebration are brown, red, orange, yellow, gold and purple.

Make incense with frankincense, sandalwood, juniper, pine, oak, honeysuckle, marigold and rose.

Decorate with gourds, pine cones, vines, seeds and sun symbols.

Samhain

Samhain is when we mark the end of the seasonal year, when we store away for the following year, when the veil between the worlds is thin and we celebrate those who have gone before us. It is a spiritual time and one that works well for divination and scrying.

The witches' new year, probably the most celebrated witches' Sabbat I would think and of course … trick or treating… and my birthday!

I love this time of the year (and not just coz of the presents…) I love autumn; the crisp fresh air, the crunch of the leaves under foot, the evenings drawing in, the promise of warm nights indoors with a good book and a big bowl of casserole.

It is a time of introspection, a time to look back over all that has occurred over the previous months. Looking at the projects that were started, ones that have worked, ones that have failed, examining them all and re-evaluating.

I always decorate the house and we do get a lot of trick or treaters. I move the furniture in my lounge so that I can put a sideboard in the bay window and I decorate it as a Samhain altar – pumpkins, cobwebs, candles, bats – all the Halloween decorations! I always dress up too.

Samhain is a good time to connect with spirit. I usually put up an ancestors altar with black and white photographs of my grandparents and great grandparents. I like to scry with water and use the crystal ball too. Along with all the decorations in the house my working altar and my main altar will also be decorated. Black altar clothes, lace, orange and black candles – I even have black roses.

I also make Mexican hot chocolate (hot milk, melted chocolate squares, cinnamon, cardamom and cloves).

Foods for Samhain – apples, gourds, nuts, squashes, pumpkin, cider, beef, pork, poultry, cakes for the dead, spices and garlic.

Colours for this celebration are orange, black, red, brown, white, gold and silver.

Make incense with mint, nutmeg, myrrh, copal, clove, basil, frankincense, lilac, yarrow and ylang ylang.

Decorate with bat symbols, black cat, spider and wolf images, ghosts, goblins, Jack-o'-lanterns, besoms and pumpkins.

The Moon

So why do we celebrate the moon and why is it so important to a witch?

The waxing moon is when the moon is a crescent in the sky and gaining her power, working her way up to becoming a full moon. Energy is building, and it is a good time to go with the flow and build up your own energy too. Touch base with friends, plan meetings and communicate.

Waxing moon magic/first quarter – good for courage, elemental magic, friends, luck and motivation. Gives vitality, courage and strength. Stimulates the heart.

The new moon is the Maiden aspect of the Goddess; a time of new beginnings, a time of possibility and opportunity. This is a wonderful time to make new beginnings of all types. It is also a good time to start something creative. New projects at work can also be launched. A good time to apply for jobs or go house hunting.

New moon magic – good for beauty, health, self-improvement; farms and gardens; job hunting; love and romance, networking. It is good for protection and creates a shield for the beginning of the cycle.

The time of the full moon is the Goddess in her full power, the tides of the seas and the energy in our own bodies are at the highest point. She is full, round and plump, she is the Mother aspect of the moon. Energies will be high at this time, so do watch out for any troubles that might raise their heads. It is a good time to work with divination and to reflect on your goals and feelings.

Full moon magic – good for artistic endeavours, beauty, health, fitness, change and decisions. Children, competition, dreams, families, health and healing, knowledge and legal undertakings. Love and romance, money, motivation, protection, psychism and self-improvement.

The waning moon is when the moon goes from full back to crescent, when she is on the descent heading towards the dark moon. The energy is waning. Follow the rhythm, clear out rubbish, de-clutter and clean the house. Follow your instincts. This is also a good time to get rid of bad habits and negative energies.

Waning moon magic/last quarter – good for addictions, divorce, health and healing, banishing disease, stress protection. Transformation from negative vibrations to positive. Balances the energy within the body and helps the mind and body flow more easily with life.

The dark moon, two days before the new moon, is the time of the Crone. A time for inner work, for reflection and introspection.

Dark moon – good for tackling addictions, change, divorce, enemies, justice, obstacles, quarrels, removal, separation, stopping stalkers and theft. Universal love of self and others. Draws love to you and removes sorrows and past hurts. Calming, protective, serene and improving relationships.

The phases of the moon are the same all over the Earth. When it is a full moon in Britain it is also a full moon in Australia, China and the United States.

Work with the phases of the moon for your spell workings; it will add power to them. You can always adjust of course, if you wanted to work a healing spell then for a waning moon you would concentrate on banishing the illness, on a waxing moon you would focus on increasing health and well being.

Observing the moon phases, celebrating them and working with the energies are ways we tune into universe, to work with deity and learn to go with the ebb and flow of energies.

The Elements

So what do we do with them?

Well, in ritual we call upon the four quarters/elements to join us, aid us and protect us. We bring all the four elements together with spirit to complete the circle. We can also call upon their powers when working spells.

Each and every person will have characteristics from each element within them and their personality. Using the four elements you can help balance yourself.

Working with the Elements

Suggestions for working with the elements; if you can't get outside to work with the elements direct, work with the crystals suggested in the chart below – meditate using them and visualize the element itself, draw a picture, or print one from the internet or look in a book at an image of the elemental for each element and meditate; research the animals that are associated with each element. Pick one or two of the scents that are associated with each element and wear them.

For each activity you do, make a mental note of how it feels, how you think you are connecting with that element, what smells there are, what you sense.

Earth: Do gardening, cook, walk in the forest, walk across fields, do mountain climbing, visit a garden or a garden centre, work with herbs, recycle, pick up litter, plunge your hands into a pot of fresh earth.

Air: Go outside when it is windy and let the air blow through you, sit on top of a hill or mountain, check the air quality in your area, and open a window. Fly a kite, watch the birds, lie on your back and watch the clouds, burn incense.

Fire: Have a bonfire or a BBQ, meditate watching a candle flame, sit and watch an open fire, watch fireworks.

Water: Go swimming, splash in puddles, walk in the rain, visit a pond or the seashore, wash the car, water the plants, take a bath or a shower and connect with the essence of water.

Earth

What comes to mind when you think about the element Earth? The first thing I think of is soil, the brown stuff I plant things into in my garden. The soil contains and stores all the minerals and moisture plants need to live. Earth is everything we are, and everything we have comes from this element. We come from it, and at the end of our lives we return to it.

No wonder the Earth element is associated with abundance and prosperity. Earth is where things grow and have their foundation. This is where the association with abundance and prosperity comes from.

Earth is also rock and stones, it makes up the foundation of our planet. It stabilises and grounds us. One of my favourite grounding exercises is to visualize myself as a tree. My roots growing down into the soft, brown soil. Wriggling my roots into it, down to the core of the very planet itself.

Earth is associated with North, with the season of winter and the advancement of old age. Winter, to me at least, is a time of reflecting. The trees and plants and even the animals have all withdrawn into Mother Earth to recuperate, to replenish, ready to venture forth in the spring, renewed and refreshed.

Don't forget to look after this element, the planet, the environment around you. It can even be something small like picking up a piece of litter.

Earth has the colours of the season of winter; those of the dark nights, brown soil, dark grassy landscape and the white of frost and snow. It is also the time of the Cailleach; she is the Goddess of Winter.

To represent this element you could use a small dish of soil, an earthenware dish, a stone, a pebble, a crystal or even a piece of wood.

Direction: North

Nature: Fertile, nurturing, stabilising, grounding

Elemental: Gnome

Colours: Green, brown, black, grey, white

Places: Caves, forests, groves, valleys, fields, farms, gardens, parks, kitchens, basements, mines, holes

Magic: Money, prosperity, fertility, stability, grounding, employment, material matters

Herbs/plants: Patchouli, vertivert, moss, nuts, roots, barley, cotton, cypress, fern, honeysuckle, horehound, knotweed, mugwort, oats, potato, primrose, rhubarb, rye, sorrel, tulip, turnip, wheat

Stones: Emerald, peridot, agate, apache tear, aventurine, orange calcite, carnelian, diamond, fluorite, jade, jasper, jet, malachite, petrified wood, ruby, sugilite, tiger eye, black or green tourmaline, unakite

Metals: Iron, lead

Animals: Dog, horse, earthworm, gopher, ant, cow, burrowing animals, wolf, bear

Season: Winter

Time: Night

Tool: Pentacle

Signs: Taurus, Virgo, Capricorn

Sense: Touch

Symbols: Salt, clay, soil, rocks, wheat, acorns

Magic type: Gardening, magnet, image, stone, tree, knot, binding

Air

What do you think of when you think of the element of Air? The image of a bright blue sky with wispy white clouds comes to my mind. The sky is limit less; you can't see an end to it.

Air is all about intellect, truth and knowledge. Air means

truth, truth in who you really are and the freedom that comes with that realisation.

Think about the qualities of the wind too, when it whips up the leaves and sends them dancing around. When a wisp of breeze catches your hair. There is nothing quite like the feeling of standing on top of a windy hill with your arms outstretched just letting the wind wrap around you. Don't forget that Air also has its destructive side, think of hurricanes and tornadoes.

Air represents East, the season of spring and youth. It is the place of hope and new beginnings. We get up, we start each new day fresh with new opportunities to learn and grow. We go out into the world to go about our business.

Spring has the same feeling – fresh, new energy. We have hibernated over winter, dreaming and planning. Now it is time to put those plans into action.

Youth is an exciting and even slightly scary time. We set out on our own, starting to explore the big world for ourselves. New experiences, new people, new ventures. This is the time when we start to discover who we are.

Air is associated with thoughts. We need Air to breath, and therefore to live. The Air we breathe in allows us to think clearly, to clear our minds.

Air has the colours of spring: yellow of the rising sun, the light blue of the sky and white of the clouds. Even pale green and pink of new foliage and blossom of Bride, the Goddess of Spring.

To represent the element of Air you might like to use feathers, incense or spring flowers.

Direction: East
Nature: Flying, moving, intelligence
Elemental: Sylph
Colours: Yellow, pale blue, pink, light green
Places: Mountain tops, plains, cloudy skies, high towers, airports, schools, libraries, offices, travel agents, psychia-

trist therapy rooms

Magic: Travel, instruction, study, freedom, knowledge, recovering lost items, creativity, visions, psychic power

Herbs/plants: Any flowers, agaric, agrimony, anise, benzoin, bergamot, bittersweet, borage, bracken, brazil nut, broom, caraway, chicory, dock, endive, fenugreek, hazel, hops, lemongrass, mace, maple, marjoram, meadowsweet, mint, mistletoe, palm, parsley, pecan, pine, rice, sage, slippery elm

Stones: Pumice, mica, amethyst, azurite, beryl, blue lace agate, carnelian, chrysoprase, citrine, diamond, fluorite, moldivite, opal, pearl, snow quartz, sapphire, sodalite, blue topaz, blue tourmaline, turquoise

Metals: Tin, copper

Animals: Spider, birds, winged insects

Season: Spring

Time: Dawn

Tool: Wand

Signs: Gemini, Libra, Aquarius

Sense: Hearing, smell

Symbols: Feathers, incense, flowers

Magic type: Divination, concentration, visualisation, wind magic

Fire

What do you think of when you think about the element of Fire? I visualize a huge bonfire, glowing red, yellow and orange or a huge pile of crackling logs and sticks. I can hear spitting sparks of flame and feel the heat on my face.

Fire brings warmth, comfort and protection. It is the light in the dark that drives away outside threats. Fire brings people together, as a community. Although most houses now don't have open fires in each room, a lot still have fireplaces. The hearth is the centre of a home.

Fire is passion; it is the burning flame inside that gives us excitement, energy and strength. It is the fire within us that helps us to meet the challenges that life brings to us. Fire also sparks our imagination, lights our desires and fills us with enthusiasm and encouragement.

Fire can also be destructive, but in that destruction comes renewal and rebirth – think of the phoenix rising from the ashes. The warning that comes with fire is that it does need to be kept in check. A fire that causes rage can get out of hand.

Cast your mind to the blacksmith's forge. The blacksmith takes raw material, heats it in the fire and creates something new from it. A transformation, this we can do with our own selves.

The fire within you is your own personal power. It is the force that gives you confidence, it takes away the fear and challenges you to push yourself that bit further.

Fire represents the South, the season of summer and adulthood. The sun is at its highest point, it is when we put all our energy into projects and help them grow and mature. The projects that were started in the spring are now flourishing. It is a time for energy, activity and passion. A time to laugh, dance, sing and have fun.

Adults have experience; experience of life and who they are. By adulthood you should have found your place in the world. You have responsibilities, control of your life and your expectations. Just remember to enjoy yourself too, find your inner passion and run with it.

Fire is the colour of summer: the reds of a beautiful sunset, the yellow of the sun and even the green and bright colours of summer flowers and plants. I think of Belenos the Celtic Sun God.

To represent Fire the most obvious item is a candle, especially a red one. You could also use a red stone/crystal.

Direction: South

Nature: Purifying, destructive, cleansing, energetic, sexual, forceful

Elemental: Salamander

Colour: Red

Places: Desert, hot spring, volcano, oven, fireplace, bedroom, locker room, sauna, sports field

Magic: Protection, courage, sex, energy, strength, authority, banishing, negativity

Herbs/plants: Stinging nettles, thistles, chillies, cacti, coffee, seeds, alder, allspice, anemone, angelica, ash, basil, bay, betony, chrysanthemum, cinnamon, clove, coriander, cumin, curry, dill, dragon's blood, fennel, carnation, carrot, cashew, cedar, fig, frankincense, garlic, ginger, hawthorn, juniper, lime, lovage, mandrake, marigold, mustard, nutmeg, oak, orange, holly, rosemary, pepper, pomegranate, tobacco, walnut, witch hazel, woodruff

Stones: Jasper, lava, quartz, amber, beryl, bloodstone, gold calcite, carnelian, citrine, coal, diamond, geodes, red jasper, obsidian, peridot, smoky quartz, rhodochrosite, sunstone, yellow topaz

Metals: Gold, brass

Animals: Snake, cricket, lizard, bee, scorpion, shark

Season: Summer

Time: Noon

Tool: Athame

Signs: Aries, Leo, Sagittarius

Sense: Sight

Symbols: Flames, lava

Magic type: Candle, storm, time, star

Water

What do you visualize when you think about the element of Water? My first thought is always of the ocean, of waves crashing on the shore.

What would we do without water, it sustains all life. Without water we and all the plants and animals would not survive. Water is very powerful – the ocean, a flood, a tidal wave.

Water is all about emotions. Emotions flow, chop and change and rise to the surface as water does in a river, lake or ocean. A shower of rain can be refreshing like the release of emotion or destructive like the waves on a rough sea.

Water is also cleansing and healing. We clean ourselves, wash our food, and clean our houses and possessions with water. Your daily household chores such as washing up can be cleansing rituals in themselves.

Water is excellent for scrying. Divination with water uses our intuition, imagination and emotions.

Take a bowl that has a dark coloured inside, fill it with water and drop a silver coin in the bottom. Calm and centre yourself, look into the water and see what images come to you.

Water represents the West. It is the season of autumn and old age. This is the time of harvest, a time to gather in. What we have spent the year nurturing and tending to is now ready to reap. It is time to let go.

As people get older and become more aware of their mortality, they seek to balance their lives. They surrender some of the hard work they have been doing and concentrate on what is most important to them. Often these are things that bring emotional fulfilment, like spending time with loved ones, or pursuing a creative dream.

Water gives us the flow of our emotions and nurtures our lives. In return, we can offer it our love. Everything we do with love, and every act of love we perform, honours Water. Love, like water, has the power of healing.

The colours of Water are the colours of the sea: the blue of the Mediterranean, and the grey of the North Sea; the black of a deep lake and the green of the sea before a storm. But also all the glorious colours of the autumn leaves that remind me of the God Mabon.

On my altar a bowl filled with sea shells represents Water.

Direction: West

Nature: Flowing, purifying, healing, soothing, loving

Elemental: Undine

Colour: Blue

Places: Lake, spring, stream, river, beach, ocean, well, swimming pool, bath, shower, fountain

Magic: Purification, love, psychic awareness, dreams, sleep, peace, marriage, friends, emotions, subconscious

Herbs/plants: Aloe, apple, aster, lemon balm, birch, blackberry, burdock, cabbage, camellia, caper, cardamom, catnip, chamomile, chickweed, coconut, coltsfoot, columbine, cowslip, cucumber, daffodil, daisy, elder, elm, eucalyptus, feverfew, gardenia, heather, hemlock, iris, larkspur, lemon, lettuce, lilac, mallow, morning glory, myrrh, pansy, peach, plum, rose, sandalwood, sea weed, tansy, thyme, tomato, valerian, water lilies, willow, yarrow, yew

Stones: Amethyst, aquamarine, blue tourmaline, beryl, calcite, chalcedony, diamond, emerald, jade, jet, kunzite, lapis lazuli, magnetite, moonstone, obsidian, onyx, opal, peridot, rose quartz, rock crystal, blue topaz, pink tourmaline, zircon

Metals: Mercury, silver, copper

Animals: Cat, frog, turtle, dolphin, whale, otter, seal, fish, shellfish

Season: Autumn

Time: Dusk

Tool: Chalice, cauldron

Signs: Cancer, Scorpio, Pisces

Sense: Taste

Symbols: Shells, water
Magic type: Sea, ice, snow, fog, mirror, magnet

Spirit/Ether

There is the fifth element, that of Spirit. To me it encompasses all the others, but here are some basic correspondences:

Direction: All four – North, East, South, West and also within, without, up and down
Nature: Everything
Colours: Purple, black
Places: Space, vacuum, voids
Metal: Meteoritic
Animals: All and none
Seasons: All and none
Time: Eternal
Magic type: Religious

Working with Energy

To really feel magic, to make spells work and to get the right result from a ritual you need ENERGY.

Every living thing has its own energy, whether it is a flower, a crystal, a person or a pebble. All of the ingredients you might gather together for a spell will have their own individual energies and characteristics. If you use a wand, that has its own energy too, but the real energy comes from YOU.

Working with energy is really a combination, you can draw energy up from the Earth or from an item such as a crystal and you channel it through yourself, but you also add a bit of energy from your inner self as you do so. When you are in ritual you might also call upon the God and Goddess to lend their energy to your workings too, you can raise energy from other sources as well. The elements can provide us with energy too – Earth, Air, Fire and Water all provide sources of energy that we can tap into.

But generally you are also the conduit, you summon the energy, you gather it, you add to it and you direct it.

Everyone has energy within them, everyone has the power to access it, to tap into it and use it. Unfortunately most people have no idea how to do so, and boy are they missing out.

The energy created by our bodies and by the spirit within our bodies is generally referred to as the aura. The energy that flows around and through our bodies is usually referred to as chi.

I would like you to try something now... yep right now... rub both your hands together (palms together) quickly for a few seconds, then very, very slowly pull them apart. Can you feel anything? You should feel a slight pull or a tingling sensation. What you can feel in between your hands is energy, that's the stuff we want to work with.

Another exercise to try is to hold your hands a couple of feet apart, palms inwards and slowly bring your hands together. You will hopefully start to feel a pressure as your hands get closer, a resistance – again this is energy. (Don't worry if you don't feel it at first, sometimes it takes some practice.)

Part of being a witch is to be connected to the Earth, her plants and her creatures, to be aware of the energies around us so that we can connect and interact with them.

You can form the energy and one of the most well used forms is the cone of power. This usually happens within a circle, the energy is raised by chanting and/or dancing in a circle, the energy builds and forms into an upwardly pointing cone that shapes itself in the centre of the circle and rises skywards. Once the cone is ready and it is felt that no more energy can be added, it is released and sent to its destination.

On a smaller scale we raise and direct energy when we work a spell, for instance a candle spell. We would take the energy from the Earth, channel it through our body and out through our hands and into a candle, this will charge the candle with energy. We add our intent and any other 'ingredients' such as herbs and oils. Once the candle is burning it releases the energy we filled it with, that energy then goes on its merry way to fulfil the intent that it was meant for.

Candle Magic

Candle magic is one of the most popular methods of working magic. It can be as simple as lighting a white candle and putting your intent into it or going the whole hog and tying in the correct colour of candle, adding corresponding herbs, anointing it with oil, carving runes or sigils, chanting a spell to go with it – or anywhere in between.

The choice is yours, it's a personal thing. Sometimes you may want to keep it simple, other times you may want to add to it – play around with all the various methods and see what works best for you.

What Type of Candle to Use?

Well, the choice is yours.

But for a candle spell you really want one that is not going to burn for days. Candles must not be left unattended, and for candle magic it is usually best to use a candle that will burn out in a short time. Tea lights are good, as are votives, small beeswax candles or even birthday cake candles.

What Colour?

A basic white candle is good and covers pretty much every intent. However, if you want to add power to your intent pick a coloured candle that mirrors your objective.

Here is a basic colour guide, but it is your choice – if a colour shouts at you to be used, go with your instinct.

Abundance – green, copper, gold
Astral travel – silver, black, purple, blue
Balance - white, silver, green, rainbow
Banishing negativity – black, white, purple
Binding – red, black

Blessing or consecrating – white, lilac, light blue
Cleansing – white
Changes – dark blue, yellow, white
Closure – black
Communication – yellow, white
Confidence – brown, orange, red, yellow
Creativity – orange, yellow
Defence – black, purple, white, dark blue
Divination – gold, lilac, yellow, black
Dreams – silver, purple, dark blue
Employment – orange, brown
Energy – gold, red
Exorcism – black, purple
Fertility – green, brown
Friendship – gold, pink, brown
Gossip, to stop – black, purple, white
Happiness – yellow, pink
Healing – light blue, yellow, pink, pale green
Love – pink, red, white
Luck – green, orange, gold
Money – green, gold
Meditation – purple, white, silver
Mental clarity – yellow, orange, white
Peace – white, black, pink, light blue
Protection – black, white, blue
Psychic powers – purple, black, white, lilac
Transformation – white, orange
Spirit contact – black, purple, lilac
Strength – red, gold, orange
Success – orange, green, gold
Truth seeking – black
Wisdom – purple, black, white

Carving

If you want to add more intent to your candle, you could carve a rune or sigil into it. Use a toothpick or a small knife and just carve your design into the candle itself. For instance, in a love candle spell you could carve a simple heart. Again this is another area where you can go with what feels right for you.

Dressing your Candle

To add even more power to your intent with your candle spell you can add scent to it, either in the form of anointing it with oil or with the addition of herbs. If you have a votive or small candle you can anoint it with your chosen oil (dip your finger in the oil and rub it on the candle from top to the middle and then bottom to the middle) and then roll it in ground up herbs. If you are using a rolled beeswax candle you can if you are very careful, warm the candle in your hand and gently unroll the beeswax then sprinkle the herbs inside and roll it back up again. If you are using a tea light you can add a few drops of your chosen oil and a sprinkle of herbs. If you have a glass votive holder you can place the candle inside and sprinkle the herbs around it.

Whilst you are anointing your candle with the oil and/or rolling it in herbs, it is important to visualize your desired outcome at the same time, again adding to the power of your intent. By 'charging' the herbs and oils as you add them to the candle you are adding power to your spell.

Below is a chart showing some of intents and the corresponding herbs to use in your candle spells, as always, go with what feels right for you. Take a look through your kitchen cupboard and spice rack – see what jumps out at you.

Astral Travel – mugwort, dittany, poplar
Confidence – borage, thyme, yarrow
Divination – broom, dandelion, meadowsweet
Dreams – jasmine, marigold, mugwort, rose

Exorcism – basil, dragon's blood, frankincense, mint, sage

Fertility – geranium, mistletoe, oak, pine, rice

Friendship – lemon, passionflower, sweet pea

Gossip, to stop – clove, slippery elm

Happiness – lavender, marjoram, oregano, meadowsweet, St John's wort

Healing – apple, lemon balm, carnation, cinnamon, garlic

Love – basil, chamomile, clove, geranium, rose

Luck – heather, nutmeg, poppy, star anise

Mental clarity – mace, mustard, rosemary

Money – basil, cinnamon, marjoram, oregano, mint, pine

Peace – lavender, vervain, meadowsweet

Protection – anise, basil, garlic, ivy, oak, sage, rice

Psychic powers – bay, cinnamon, mugwort, anise, thyme, yarrow

Spirit contact – dandelion, sweetgrass, thistle, wormwood

Success – lemon balm, cinnamon, ginger, rowan

Wisdom – beech, dandelion, hazel, sage, sandalwood

Also use the elements – if you are using your candle for a spell involving emotions, how about a floating candle in a small dish of water, or standing a small bottle of spring water by the candle? If your spell is for grounding, stand the candle in some soil. Use your imagination, and go with whatever inspiration takes you.

If you work with tarot, how about picking a corresponding tarot card and standing it by your candle as it works its magic?

You could also add a small crystal chip to the base of the candle, pressing it into the wax.

Another idea is to surround your candle once it is in its holder with corresponding crystals, adding more energy, power and intent.

Below is a chart outlining some intents and the corresponding crystals to use in your candle spells, but, as always, go with your own instinct:

Abundance – agate, citrine, amazonite

Astral travel – sugilite, opal, jasper, hematite

Balance – bloodstone, rhodochrosite, yellow calcite

Banishing negativity – amber, amethyst, obsidian, tiger's eye, hematite

Blessing or consecrating – quartz, amethyst

Cleansing – mossy agate, amethyst, jade

Changes – snowflake obsidian

Divination – moonstone, quartz

Empowering – amber, quartz

Fertility – green jasper

Happiness – malachite, chrysacolla

Healing – sugilite, agate, selenite

Love – rose quartz

Luck – amazonite

Manifesting – sugilite, amber, kyanite

Money – malachite, pyrite, tourmaline

Meditation – fluorite, sodalite, snow quartz

Protection – malachite, dolomite, bloodstone, amethyst

Psychic powers – quartz, selenite

Transformation – amethyst, moldavite

Spirit contact – amethyst, black obsidian

Strength – bloodstone, diamond, mossy agate

Success – carnelian, citrine, malachite, aventurine

Wisdom – tiger's eye, ruby, jade, lapis lazuli, sapphire

Pinning your Candle

You can also use a straight pin in your candle spell. This is where you place a pin into your candle at the spot where the magic will be released. Once the candle burns down to the pin and releases it the spell is done.

When Should I Work Candle Magic?

Well, again this is up to you. If you have a need to do the

working right now... then do it. If you want to add a bit of oomph to your candle magic working then you could correspond it to the phase of the moon.

The basic rule of thumb with the moon phases is:

Waxing moon is for growth and new projects.
Full moon is for completions, healing and empowerment.
Waning moon is for releasings, cleansings and banishings.
New (or dark) moon is for divination.

If you really want to get specific, you could also perform the candle magic on the corresponding day of the week:

Sunday – success, promotion, leadership, pride, light, fitness and personal growth. This is for achievements of any kind – fame, wealth, and acknowledgement. Health issues, increasing your personal power and sticking to diets all fall under Sunday.

Monday – inspiration, illusion, prophetic dreams, emotions, psychic abilities, travel, women's mysteries and fertility – well it is the moon's day after all.

Tuesday – bravery, honour, courage along with passion and strength to fight the good fight. Work on increasing all these things.

Wednesday – communication skills, cleverness, intelligence, creativity, business sense, writing, artistic talents, music, the arts and crafts. Seek the wisdom and improvement of your skills.

Thursday – prosperity, abundance, leadership and good health. Take the power of Thor's day and work with it!

Friday – well it is Freya's day so it's got to be love, fertility, romance and beauty magic, with happiness and friendship thrown in for good measure.

Saturday – Saturn's day, a God of the passage of time and karma. Saturday is a good day to work on protection, removing obstacles, binding and banishing negativity.

Clean up day – clear out any problems.

Do I Need to Cast a Circle for Candle Magic?

Now I know you are probably fed up with hearing this by now, but it is your choice. Generally I don't bother if I am doing the spell working at home as my house is regularly smudged and protected. However, if you are dealing with spirit, or negative energies then I would say it is a wise precaution. It doesn't have to be an elaborate ritual with quarter calling and bell ringing. Walk deosil around the area you are going to be doing your working in, visualize a bright, white light forming a circle, then forming a dome around you. When you have finished your working, walk widdershins around the area visualizing the protective circle dissipating.

What about the Spell Itself?

If you are good with words then a short chant works well, rhyming is good too. Make sure your intent is clearly stated; make sure it is worded correctly with no room for misinterpretation. I usually end my spells with 'an harm to none' just to make sure I am covered. Decide if you want to make it a long chant or a short one, a short one can always be chanted several times over. There are plenty of spells in books and on the internet; I have included some here as well. However, personally I feel that a spell will work much better if it is personalised for you. So if you use a spell written by someone else, how about just tweaking it a bit so that it has that added bit of you in it?

Then What?

Well, you have got your candle, you have dressed it if you wished, you picked the day and moon phase (again if you wished), then what happens?

Set the candle in a suitable holder; place any other items around it – crystals, tarot cards etc if that is what you have decided upon.

Settle yourself comfortably in front of the candle. Take a few deep breaths to centre yourself. Light the candle and start with your spell or chant. As you say the words focus your intent in your mind. Visualize what you want to happen, how you want the spell to work. Send the energy of your intent into the candle itself.

When you have finished your chant and your visualization, leave the candle to burn itself out.

Now What Do I Do?

Take the candle stub and any remains of burnt herbs etc and dispose of them. Burying them in the garden is good. If you have used any crystals it is a good idea to cleanse them – under running water, with salt or incense or however you prefer to do so.

Then let the universe do its work. However, if you have worked a spell to gain something you want – a job, a new love etc. You may have to do some leg work yourself. If you are after a new job but haven't actually got out into the world and looked for one then it's not going to happen. Even magic needs a helping hand sometimes ;-)

I also like to give a little offering after working magic, even just to water the garden, feed the plants or leave some food out for the birds.

Candle Magic Prosperity Spell

What you will need:

A green candle
Optional herbs & crystals:
Jasmine or jasmine essential oil (for money)
Poppy seeds (for money & luck)
Pine needles or pine essential oil (for money)

Malachite (for money & success)
Green tourmaline (money)

What you do:

Dress your candle with the oils/herbs. Place it in a holder and put the crystals around the base.
Light the candle and focus on the intent.
Say three times:

Lord & Lady help us to be
Good with finances and money
Guide us to financial good
Abundance, prosperity and guidance should
From financial worry set us free
And harm to none, so mote it be

Allow the candle to burn out.

Candle Magic Spell for Strength, Courage and Confidence

What you will need:

Red candle
Herbs/oils & crystals:
Allspice (courage)
Rosemary (strength)
Yarrow (courage)
Red jasper (negativity & strength)
Garnet (self esteem & confidence)
Tigers eye (self confidence)

What you do:

This spell needs to be worked on a Tuesday or a Sunday.

Dress the candle with the oils/herbs. Place the crystals around the candle.

Say three times:

On this Mars day there is fiery energy to spare
For ...(insert name here)... I call for courage and self confidence
To know, to will, to dare
Three stones and a burning candle of red
I call for him/her, bravery and banish fear and dread
For the good of all, with harm to none
By Mars energy, this spell is done

Allow the candle to burn out.

Candle Magic Spell for Protection for your Job

What you will need:

Black candle
Herbs/oils/crystals:
Rosemary (protection)
Ivy (protection)
Sage (protection, wishes)
Malachite (business success, protection, hope)
Jasper (protection)
Quartz (protection)
Tigers Eye (luck, protection)

What you do:

Dress the candle with the herbs/oils. Place the stones around the base of the candle.

Say three times:

Crystals and stones of protection and power

Lend... (insert name here)... your strength and protection in this
   magic hour
Safety and security this spell now yields
As we increase our energy and boost our shields
Health, wisdom and protection now do I call
In all seasons, winter to spring and summer to fall
For the good of all, with harm to none
By all the powers of three times three,
As I will it, then so shall it be!

Allow the candle to burn out.

Candle Magic Spell for Happiness

What you need:

A tea light or a yellow candle
Herbs/oils/crystals:
Feverfew (protection)
Red rose petals (love, healing, luck)
Yellow rose petals (happiness, success)
Rosemary (love, protection, healing)
Lavender (love, happiness, peace)
Rose quartz (peace, love, comfort, companionship)
Malachite (hope, happiness)

What you do:

Dress the candle with the herbs/oils. Take each stone in your
   hand and charge them with your intent, then place the
   stones around the base of the candle. Light the candle.
Say three times:

With the grace of Eros, Aphrodite and Freya
Please lift this grey veil of despair

Fill ...(insert name here)... life with happiness and light
To benefit them, family and friends with delight
An harm to none, so mote it be!

Leave the candle to burn out.

Candle Magic Spell to Deflect and Banish Negativity

What you need:

A thin black candle (a taper one)
An envelope or paper bag

What you do:

Sit in front of the candle and say:

On this day, this candle spell takes place
Fear and dread be gone, I banish you from time and space

Light the black candle.
Visualize all the negativity and problems that need to be safely removed from your life.
Say:

This black candle represents all the negativity
With magic I break the bad luck that is surrounding me

Pinch out the candle flame and then snap the candle in half.
Say:

By the powers of the moon, the stars and the sun
As I will, so mote it be and let it harm none

Put the broken candle in the bag/envelope. Close it and put a drip of candle wax on it to seal the spell. Remove the bag from your property. Dispose of it. Once done, turn your back and don't look back. Put it all behind you.

The Crafts

Natural Magic Blessing for the Heart of the Home

What you will need:

Small dish of salt to represent the Earth and prosperity
Incense to represent Air and knowledge
A red candle for fire and courage
Small bowl of water to represent water and love

What you do:

Straighten the room.
Light the candle and the incense.
Place the candle in the centre of the room.
Begin in the East moving deosil work around the room; first sprinkle a little salt in each corner. Then carry the incense round waving the smoke to help it flow. Next sprinkle a little water around the perimeter of the room.
Then settle in front of the candle and visualize the blessings from each of the four elements.
Prosperity from deep in the Earth.
Knowledge in the fragrant breeze from the Air.
Courage from the flame of Fire.
Love from the Water.
Picture these gifts and visualize you and your family receiving them equally.
Centre yourself.
Say this blessing:

Elements four I call, release now your power
As I bless my home in this magical hour
No negativity can enter, no spirit shall roam

As I consecrate and protect the heart of my home

As you finish the charm, draw a circle in the air above the candle flame with your finger. Spiral it up faster and faster, higher and higher, until you fling the energy off and out into the form.

Then close the spell by saying:

This home is now blessed by my will and desire
I close this spell by Earth, Air, Water and Fire

Allow the candle and incense to burn out.

Spiritual Washes and Smudges

You and your home can attract all sorts of energies and vibrations, so I think it is good practice to routinely have a spiritual clear out.

It isn't just the magic that you work within your home that will bring in energies, everything that comes from outside will bring its own energies with it. For instance, your grocery shopping will have been held and touched by many people, each one adding their own energies to it, and they won't always be good energies.

So Let's Clean House!

Salt is particularly good for spiritual house cleaning. Sprinkle a little in the corners of each room for purification and protection.

Smudging – this can be done with a bunch of dried sage, dried rosemary, dried lavender, sweet grass (or a combination) or even with your favourite incense. You can either start at your front door or in the centre of your home, but work your way around your house, going into each room and wafting the smoke around, making sure it gets into all the corners. You can use a chant whilst you are doing this, asking any negative energy to leave and to be replaced with positive, loving and happy energy.

Housework – yes I know this is really boring. But the accumulation of dust, rubbish and mess in a home can cause negative energies. Clutter in the house can cause chaos in the atmosphere.

You can clean out the negative energy by sweeping with a besom, sweeping from the front of the house to the back and sending out any negativity. You can even add a few drops of essential oil to the bristles of your broom to help.

You can make your own cleansing and purifying mist by using a spray bottle filled with distilled water (boil the water in your kettle and let it cool) and adding a few drops of essential oil to it and popping a rosemary, sage or lavender sprig into the bottle. Rose water, frankincense, cinnamon and lavender are all good for this purpose.

Once you have done the general housework you can use spiritual cleansers such as floor washes. These washes can also be used on worktops too.

All-Purpose Floor Wash
What you will need:

6 drops rosemary essential oil
6 drops pine needle essential oil

You can also add geranium or orange oil to give it a bit of spiritual uplift too. Or come up with your own essential oil combinations.

Add the wash to your bucket of water and start mopping.

Florida Water
In hoodoo the use of Florida Water, an American version of Cologne Water, is common in households; it brings in good spirits and honours the ancestors.

What you will need:

16 ozs distilled water
¼ cup vodka
6 drops lavender essential oil
2 drops clove essential oil
8 drops bergamot essential oil

You can also hang bunches of dried herbs above door ways to bring certain intents to the house. Rosemary, bay and thyme are good all-rounders for protection, lavender is good for a happy home, chilli peppers keep out hexes and cinnamon brings good spiritual vibes to a home.

Room spray – using a spray bottle and a base of distilled water (boiled and cooled kettle water) add 12 to 21 drops of essential oil to half a cup of water.

Some recipes ideas:

Chase Away House Cleansing Spray
½ cup distilled water
9 drops lavender oil
9 drops myrrh oil
3 drops rosemary oil

Soul Heal Spray
9 drops geranium oil
9 drops palmarose oil
3 drops lime oil

For Prosperity
Wrap up a silver coin and a basil leave in a piece of paper and pop it under your front door mat to bring prosperity into the house.

Cleansing the Spiritual You
The spiritual cleansing and blessing extends from the home to

you with bath salt and sachet blends, herbal soaps, oils and waters. All can be made and used with specific intents.

Bath Crystals
2 cups (250g) sea salt or sea salt crystals
1 cup (125g) Epsom salts
¼ teaspoon of essential oil – a combination that works for you, experiment.

Body Powder Base

2 tablespoons baking soda
5 tablespoons arrowroot or cornstarch
1 tablespoon ground orris root

Then add ground herbs and essential oils of your choice – dried orange peel, marigold petals, lemon balm, neroil oil, lavender buds and oils – use the herbs and scents that balance with your intent.

Four Thieves Vinegar
In 1772 during the plague, four thieves made a habit of robbing graves of the dead and stealing their precious items. As they came from a family of perfumers they knew the properties of herbs, so made a garlic-infused vinegar to rub on their bodies to protect them from the plague. Although thankfully we no longer have to worry about the plague, the 'four thieves vinegar' is useful for protection if applied to the body and for immunity when taken (1/2 teaspoon of the vinegar mix to 8oz water). If you don't fancy using the garlic you could replace that with an antibacterial or antiseptic herb such as rosemary or sage.
What you will need:

16 oz cider vinegar or white vinegar

4 cloves garlic

Mince the garlic, add a drop of the vinegar to it and mash until soft. Spoon the garlic into a sterilised jar or bottle and pour on the rest of the vinegar. Swirl daily for three to four weeks. You could make up a chant whilst you swirl, along the lines of sending evil on its way and keeping you protected.

Witch-Bottles

I love using Witch-bottles, I always have a couple on the go in my house for protection, clearing out negative energies and bringing happiness to the home.

Again these are so easy to make, you don't need special pretty bottles you can just use old clean jam jars. Mine are in old jam jars so I tuck them away under furniture, but if you do have some pretty bottles you could decorate them and make them a feature.

Generally speaking, the modern day Witch-bottles are very similar to historical Witch-bottles in their basic structure, even though their intended purpose has changed. The most common purpose for constructing a Witch-bottle today is capturing negative energies targeted at the constructor of the bottle, her family or her home. Some Witch-bottles are intended to change negative energy into positive energy and then release it into the surrounding area.

The basic structure of Witch-bottles can be used for purposes other than protective: for financial gain, for helping with artistic creativity, to call forth positive energy, for improving health, etc.

Basically a Witch-bottle is a container of some sort, usually a jar or a bottle, which is filled with objects that fulfil a given magical purpose. The person making the Witch-bottle or, in other words, the one casting the bottled spell, can charge the objects magically beforehand and build the bottle to work on this charging until the need of renewing the spell arises. Witch-bottles can also be built to recharge themselves by the energy they 'capture' for as long as the bottle stays unbroken, whether it is years or centuries.

The typical contents of the basic protective Witch-bottle today are quite similar to that of the traditional one: nails, sand or different coloured sands, crystals, stones, knotted threads, herbs, spices, resin, flowers, candle wax, incense, votive candles, salt, vinegar, oil, coins, saw dust, ashes etc. Actually, everything used in 'normal spells' can be used in this bottled version of a spell, the Witch-bottle.

Original witch bottles were used to keep witches away. They also used to contain all sorts of bodily fluids, hair and finger nail clippings – you can still use these if you wish.

Basically, start with your jar or bottle, then charge each item before you add it, layering up the ingredients as you go.

It really is up to you what you put in. I like to put in three nails to attract negativity and for protection. I also put in a piece of string with three knots in, knotting in my intent with each tie. If it is for prosperity I often drop in a silver coin. I usually put salt in for protection, cleansing and purification. I also like to add some kind of dried pulse – lentils or beans to soak up any negative energy. Garlic is good for protection too. Then add any herbs, spices and flowers that correspond with your intent – rose petals for love, cinnamon for success, mint and basil for prosperity etc. Keep filling the jar or bottle up until you reach the top then put the lid on. If I am using a jam jar I like to draw a pentacle on the lid. If I am using a bottle with a cork I like to seal the cork lid with dripped wax.

If you are making the Witch-bottle for protection for your own home you might like to put in a pebble from the garden, a couple of fallen leaves from the tree in your yard and a bit of cobweb from inside the house, it makes it all more personal and ties the bottle to the energies of the home. This also gives me a good excuse for having cobwebs in the house. I need them for the Witch-bottles…

A twist on the Witch-bottle is a money jar.

Use a clean, cleansed jar and half fill it with rice or seeds (fenugreek seeds are good). As you half fill the jar visualize prosperity and abundance. Then every day add two more seeds to the jar, visualising prosperity as you do. When the jar is full bury the seeds whilst sending up a request to deity that your desire will be fulfilled.

You can also do this with a jar and your loose change, each time you drop a couple of coins in the jar visualize prosperity, every so often sprinkle in a few herbs that correspond with prosperity such as basil or mint. When the jar is full you can count it up and use it for something special. You can also decorate the jar with runes that symbolise prosperity and abundance.

Witches' Ladders

One of the most well known charms using feathers is the Witches' Ladder. This is another all-purpose charm that can be worked in different colours, with different beads and charms added for different intents.

To make a Witches' Ladder, use three cords, yarns, strings or ribbons and braid them together, use colours that correspond with your intent if you would like to. As you braid, charge the cords with your intent, as you work through the braid add in beads, bells and charms if you wish.

The Witches' Ladder can be made to any length that suits you. Once it is finished, slip feathers in between the braids. As you add each feather state your intent. You can also slip pieces of herb into the braids too.

Incense

Loose incense is extremely easy to make.

Start with a base, a resin is good such as frankincense or copal. Adding a wood of some sort helps your incense to burn longer too. Use something like sandalwood, or if you are using home grown dried herbs the woody stems of herbs can be added in too. Then the choice is up to you, whether you go for the scent you like or for the intent. Incense can be made for prosperity, love, success etc, but you can also make incense to correspond with the moon phase, a Sabbat, a particular ritual or to honour a specific deity.

I also like to add a few drops of essential oil to my incense mix once I have finished it too, just to give it an extra boost of scent and power.

Remember as well that incense put together for magical purpose may not always smell particularly pleasant, it is the energies of the herbs that are important.

I would also suggest keeping it simple. Too many ingredients and it gets complicated. Less is more as they say.

So, pick you base resin and/or wood, tying them into your intent, and then add your herbs, spices and flowers – keep them corresponding to your intent. If you are making an incense to represent the element of Air you would choose herbs that relate to that element such as anise, lavender and mint perhaps. If you were making incense to honour the Goddess you might use lemon balm, geranium and thyme as these are all feminine herbs.

Don't forget that loose incense burnt on charcoal makes quite a bit of smoke.

Incense cones and sticks can be made fairly easily. Put together the ingredients you want and then grind them into a very, very fine powder. Make sure it is really fine otherwise it won't stick together. Then the choice is yours as to what you use to stick it all together, you can use gum Arabic, makko or tragacanth mixed with charcoal or saltpetre to aid combustion. (Please note that saltpetre is a toxic substance).

Incense pellets are easy to make, but again you will need to add something to help them stick together. Labdanum is often used (sometimes called neriko). Simply combine all your ingredients then add the labdanum bit by bit until it becomes a suitable consistency. Honey can also be used to stick your dry ingredients together to form pellets.

Here are some of my favourite incense recipes (use equal amounts of each ingredient).

Across the Veil Incense

Cinnamon
Honeysuckle
Marigold
Mugwort
Frankincense resin

Heaping on the Happy Incense

Basil
Fir
Lavender
Orange
Copal resin

Cleanse & Release Incense

Frankincense resin
Clove
Lavender
Cedar
Rose

Medicine Bags

Medicine bags, gris gris or mojo bags are fabulous to work with. (All different names for pretty much the same thing).

A medicine bag contains items that are charged with your intent and each item is a guide for the spirits to help them understand what the outcome you desire is. Your medicine bag once it is put together is essentially 'alive' with energy and it will need to be looked after and 'fed' with magic powder (instructions below). You will need to feed it periodically to maintain its energy force.

Africans call the power of nature 'ashe' and this is what is present in all herbs, plants and stones – in fact anything from nature. It is this power that we are using within the medicine bags.

A medicine bag can contain all sorts of items – herbs, roots, spices, crystals, feathers, bones, shells, dirt, pebbles, coins – what you put in your medicine bag is up to you.

I also want to mention here a hoodoo practice called Nation Sacks. This for women only (sorry guys). Men aren't even allowed to touch a woman's Nation Sack otherwise he will meet with bad luck. A Nation Sack is basically a protection aid for women and children. I think part of the power of these is the secrecy behind them. They are also sometimes used to draw love and can be extremely powerful, a love Nation Sack will often contain herbs and crystals, but will also hold hair, photographs and fingernail clippings.

I like the idea of a Nation Sack; I don't have one myself but I have a variation on the idea and use a medicine pouch. It is a small leather bag I made and I put things in it that I need at the time. It might contain herbs, crystals, a small bone, shells, feathers – anything that I feel the need of and I wear it when I am in ritual.

Traditional gris gris bags use red flannel for the bag itself, but I like to add colour magic to my medicine bags, I use orange material a lot as this is the colour for success, but also using green for prosperity, blue for healing etc works really well. You don't even have to be good at sewing, just use a handkerchief (do people still use these?), or felt is good as that doesn't need hemming, or just use a scrap of material. It can be tied with string or ribbon, but remember you need to get into it regularly to feed it. You can also use the chiffon bags that craft shops sell for

wedding favours. Be creative...
  Some ideas for you:

Fast Luck

Use green material for the bag and add:

  Feathers
  Nutmeg – for luck
  A red lodestone
  6 silver coins

Stay Away

Use orange or black material for the bag and add:

  Rosemary
  Pinch of dirt (graveyard dirt is good for this)
  Pinch of dried dragon's blood
  A black onyx

Love Drawing

Use red or pink material for the bag and add:

  Rose petals
  Lemon balm
  Stick of cinnamon
  Rose quartz
  A sea shell

Magic Powders

And now on to the magic powder to feed your medicine bag, although magic powders also have lots of other uses. They can be used to roll candles in for spell work, to sprinkle around your house for protection, to add oomph to rituals and any spells, to add to poppets and Witches-Bottles or to wear in a small bottle as a charm.

To make a magic powder the ingredients you use must be ground so you will need either a pestle and mortar or the end of a rolling pin and a solid bowl.

As you add each ingredient to the bowl charge it first with your intent. I also like to charge the powder as a whole once it is complete too.

This can then be fed to your medicine bag each week, just a sprinkle; you can even boost the power by feeding it on the corresponding day of the week to your intent. Or keep it in an airtight bottle or jar to use for all sorts of other spell work.

I like to use a base for my magic powders. I usually use either salt or sugar, as it grinds well and adds its own qualities to the mix too. If I am making faery wishes powder I also like to add in a little bit of glitter.

A popular hoodoo recipe is for Hot Foot Powder; this can be used to keep enemies or bullies away and is good for protecting your property too.

Hot Foot Powder Basic Recipe

½ cup (65g) cayenne pepper
½ cup (65g) salt
½ cup (65g) ground black pepper

Use a suitable chant as you grind the powder together with your intent.

Sprinkle in the footsteps of your enemies to keep them away, or spread around the perimeter of your house to keep out unwanted people or thieves.

You can vary the mixture by adding red peppercorns, or chilli powder.

Fast Luck

Ground nutmeg
Ground cinnamon
Sugar for sweet success
Lemon balm

Stay Away

Mustard powder
Salt
Rosemary
Garlic powder

Love Drawing

Lavender
Ginger
Marjoram
Sugar

Offerings

An offering is easy peasey to make, you can use whatever herbs, spices, wood chips, crystals you want. Just mix them up as you would incense, grind to a powder if you so wish and then sprinkle on the ground by your favourite tree, in your garden, at the seashore – wherever you feel works best for your intent.

You can also make offerings out of salt dough.

4 cups (500g) flour
1 cup (125g) salt
1 ½ cups (350ml) hot water
1 tsp vegetable oil

Preparation:

Combine the salt and flour, then add the water until the dough becomes elastic. Add the oil at this stage and knead the dough (if it's too sticky, add more flour). Once it's a good consistency you are ready to create.

For offering balls, take a golf ball size amount of dough and make a well in the centre with your thumb then you can add herbs, whatever you have or want to add, you can tie them in with your intent. Then form the dough into a ball around the herbs. You can add a crystal chip into the top of the ball if you wish.

A variation on this is to roll the dough out and use cookie cutters to make shapes, cut two shapes and put some herbs in between, moisten the edges with water and stick the two dough shapes together sealing the herbs inside.

Bake in the oven at 200C until hard (about 20 - 30 minutes); keep an eye on them so they don't burn.

You can then use them as offerings when you are out in the woods, fields or at the sea as they are safe to leave outside, they are all natural and will bio degrade back into the Earth.

This dough recipe can also be used to make dough wreaths for the Sabbats, just separate into three and roll out into long strands, plait together and join into a circle. You can then cookie stamp out flowers or leaves and stick them to the plaited wreath with a little water. When it is baked you can paint and varnish it if you wish.

Ink

It is a lovely idea to write your spells and chants in your Book of Shadows with magical ink, and it is so easy to make.

You will need some coloured ink, red, green, purple the choice is yours. Then just add a drop or two of your favourite essential oil to the ink and give it a stir (not too much otherwise it will be too oily). You can also tie in the choice of essential oil with the intent if you are using the ink to write a spell.

Poppets

I know what you might be thinking – eeeek that's scary voodoo stuff. But don't worry, it isn't, I promise. We have Hollywood and the media to thank for that bad (and inaccurate press).

The use of poppet dolls in sympathetic magic is ancient, going back to the days of ancient Egypt. The enemies of Ramses III made wax poppets of the Pharaoh to bring about his death. OK that did involve some not very nice magic. but it wasn't all like that, I did promise didn't I?

Ancient Greeks used poppets to protect against negative spirits or to bind two lovers together.

West African slaves used poppets containing spirits to be carried with them as protective talismans.

Poppets are used in hoodoo and folk magic for all sorts of purposes, think of the poppet as a convenient and charming package for holding your spell, be it for love, luck, prosperity, healing or protection, for pretty much any use you can think of really.

Your poppet can be as simple as a few pieces of twine twisted together to form a stick man shape or elaborately dressed and decorated dollies or anything in between. You can make them from scratch using natural twigs, string, felt, scraps of material or you can purchase a doll in a store to dress up, the choice is yours.

I tend to make my poppets from felt. It is relatively inexpensive, comes in all sorts of colours, doesn't fray at the edges and is easy to cut and sew. I like to use felt because it means I can use colour magic as well, corresponding the colour felt I use with the intent of the poppet. I use a simplified 'gingerbread' man shape (as if he is standing with both legs together, so he has a head, two arms, a torso and effectively one big fat leg). Cut out two shapes (a front and a back). Sew a button for one eye and a cross stitch for the other, or two cross stitch eyes and a mouth. Cut out a small heart shape in felt and sew that on in the correct heart area. Put both sides together and sew round the edges, it doesn't have to be neat, and it doesn't have to be perfect. Leave a gap for stuffing.

Then you have to decide what to stuff him with. This will be according to what your intent is and to a certain extent what herbs, spices and plants you have to hand. So for a healing poppet I might fill him with lavender, lemon balm and carnation petals.

I charge each herb with my intent before I use it as stuffing. Then when he is full I sew up the gap. I charge the complete poppet once more with the intent and he is done.

The poppet can be placed on an altar, carried with you for protection or, in hoodoo, a poppet is often buried in the ground to work its magic.

Pendulums

All you need to make your own pendulum is a piece of string, ribbon or cord and something to hang on the end of it. A hag stone works well (a stone with a hole in the middle); a gold or silver ring works too, even a small piece of wood with a hole drilled through it.

Runes

Runes are easy to make. If you have access to the seashore you can collect small round pebbles, all of similar sizes, and paint a rune on each one. They last longer if you give them a quick coat of varnish. You can also use the small round glass pebbles that florists use in vases, some of them come in really pretty colours.

Fehu – advance projects, used to send energy of other runes, temporary changes, material wealth

Uruz – enhances strength, sends courage

Thurisaz – breakthroughs, defence, change

Ansuz – wisdom, eloquence, inspiration, sending information

Raido – protection in astral or physical travel, getting something to move ahead

Kano – creating an opening, banishment, illumination, fire magic

Gebo – creating balance, healing, bonding energies, Air magic

Wunjo – wish rune, success, binds group energies in a positive way

Hagalaz – overcoming obstacles, banishing, blessing, defence activities

Nauthiz – seeking freedom, finding liberation, turning a bad situation good, turning away enemies

Isa – blocking negative energy, freezing a situation, finding clarity, binding negativity

Jera – harvesting what you have done, bringing rewards you have earning, improving a situation

Eihwaz – attuning energies, hunter rune, achieving true aims, finishing projects, closure

Perth – understanding a situation, initiation, secrets, vision questing, shamanistic work, fate

Algiz – protection, luck, defence, psychic abilities

Sowelu – bringing about victory, success, healing, making wise choices

Teiwaz – justice, honour, victory, order, courage

Berkana – starting a new project, fertility, purification, motherhood, reincarnation

Ehwaz – partnerships, overcoming obstacles within a group, psychic abilities with others

Mannaz – intelligence, career and school work, arbitration

Laguz – dreams, psychic phenomena, fascinations, glamouries

Inguz – focus, grounding, opportunities, calming

Othila – prosperity, finding fortunate influences

Dagaz – positive outlook, finding balance and harmony, transformation

Spirit Animal Stones

Each animal has its own characteristics and from those we can learn and use those skills and energies. Use an animal spirit stone to honour your totem animal, to use a particular animal's energies or to use those energies in a spell.

Spirit stones combine the healing properties of the stones themselves. A stone can absorb negative energy and convert it into positive energy, added with an image of the animal itself brings in the energies of that creature.

Use pebbles from the beach or from the garden, cleanse them and paint an image of the animal on, it doesn't have to be amazing artwork just a representation. Once you have done the image, charge the stone with the characteristics of that particular animal.

Magical Gardening

It doesn't matter if you only have a window sill with a pot plant on it, a small city patio, a playing field or several acres, you can always work with the magic in your garden.

Being in regular contact with your garden and what you grow, even with your house plants or a few pots of herbs, can help you to connect with the spirit of nature and recognise the subtleties of the changing of the seasons. Your garden can also provide you with food and magical ingredients.

Magical gardening does take time, focus and attention. You can't just plant something and leave it in the hope that several months later it will have grown, flourished and be covered in fruit or flowers (OK on the odd occasion it does happen, but not often).

Although I live in the city I do have a small walled garden and I love it. I have some shrubs, lots of roses, lots of bedding plants in pots and hanging baskets in the summer, loads of herbs – all in pots, and several climbers. It is enough to keep me busy.

In the summer the pots need watering every day, the flowers need regular dead heading and towards the end of the summer I also collect a lot of seeds. The herbs need regular picking during the summer months, this not only gives me a good harvest but also encourages the plant to continue growing. I also dry a lot of herbs and flowers for magical use. In the autumn everything gets cut back and tidied up ready for the winter.

Over the winter months the garden pretty much looks after itself, I just pop out there to feed the birds. As spring approaches I go out more regularly to tidy up and keep a check on the new items as they start to show their faces to the world.

The time I spend in the garden is a good way for me to connect with nature, with the Divine and to ground and centre myself at the end of the day. The garden is a good place for spotting the Fae. It is also the place I escape to when I need somewhere to myself.

My garden is where I stand in the dark to soak up the energies of the moon and it is where I stand in the daylight to soak up the energies of the sun. It is where my small chimenea stands that I use for any spells that require items to be burnt. It is where I go to meditate when it is dry. It is my haven.

I also believe that growing your own herbs and flowers to use for magical purposes adds some of your own energy into them before you use them in a working – a little extra oomph.

Harvesting and using my own herbs and flowers for magical workings also guarantees that they haven't been sprayed with all sorts of chemicals and pesticides too.

My garden is also filled with all sorts of things that aren't plants, I have beautiful wind chimes that help me when I meditate in the garden. I have a bird table and several bird feeders hanging in a small tree, feeding the birds not only helps care for the animals on this planet of ours, but I think it is also a way of honouring deity. I have pretty sparkly strings of beads hanging around too; these are there to look pretty, but also to attract the Fae. The back wall of my garden is painted with the shape of the mother Goddess and has sun and moon plaques hung around it.

From Outdoors to Indoors

The easiest way to bring some magic into the house or the home from nature's garden is with fresh flowers or a pot plant. Not only will it look beautiful and be a connection for you to the spirit of nature, but each flower and plant also has magical properties of its own that it can bring to your home.

Let's have a look at the properties of some of the more usual house plants:

African violet – spirituality and protection

Spider plant – absorbs negative energies

Fern – protection

Ivy – fidelity and fertility

Aloe – not only good to have to hand in the kitchen for burns it is also a plant of luck and wards against accidents

Ficus – love, luck, guards against hunger

Cyclamen – fertility, happiness and lust (a good one for the bedroom)

Pansy – to ease matters of the heart (folk name heartsease)

Carnations – health and healing

Marigolds – psychic abilities

Roses – lust, love and romance

With roses especially you can also add colour magic to the properties, so white roses would bring peace, yellow would bring happiness, orange would bring energy etc.

There are many, many shrubs and ground cover plants and all of them have magical properties such as hydrangeas, which are good for hex breaking, or lilacs and viburnum, both of which are good for protection. The periwinkle is a pretty ground cover plant that not only attracts the Fae, but is also excellent in spells for bindings, protection, love and prosperity.

But don't take my word for what magical properties each of the plants in your garden have, use your own intuition and 'spidery senses' to see what properties you think your plants have.

Flowers

Not only beautiful to look at and a source of nectar for the bees, flowers are incredibly special when it comes to magic. I think there are probably flowers of every single shade and colour – and again here you can use your colour magic to work with them. Blue flowers can be used to represent the element of water, purple ones would be good for psychic abilities and power, pink flowers for love and friendship etc.

Of course each specific type of flower has its own magical meaning too. Flowers also have a language of their own dating back to Victorian times, when the flower that was given to you by a friend or intended had its very own message – forget-me-not would mean 'true love', daisy would mean 'innocence' and thistle would mean 'I will never forget thee', although I am not sure about some of the messages personally, such as sage meant 'domestic virtues' and daffodil meant 'delusive hope'.

There are also flowers associated with each month, which can be used in your magical workings. Whether you use the correspondence to tie in with the date you are working the spell or the month of birth for the person you are working the spell for, it will add power to it.

This is a very basic guide to give you the idea, but again go with what feels right to you.

January – crocus, snowdrop
February – primrose
March – daffodil
April – daisy, sweet pea
May – broom, rose
June – lavender, yarrow
July – jasmine
August – sunflower, marigold
September – lily
October – dahlia
November – chrysanthemum
December - Poinsettia

Herbs

I think herbs are an important part of magical gardens. Even if you don't have a garden at all you usually have a window sill that can house a pot of herbs.

There are many types of herb, some hardy some not. You will need to check which ones can grow outside and which ones suit your soil and area. I can't grow basil very well outside, it doesn't like our climate very much and I can't seem to grow parsley at all – but that is probably down to the folk tale that if a woman is in charge of the household parsley won't grow in the garden...

Deity

Lots of flowers and plants have associations with specific deities. If you work with a particular God or Goddess you could put a plant in your garden that they would appreciate. For instance cyclamen, willow and monkshood are associated with Hecate, roses and heather with Isis, violets and roses with Aphrodite.

Flower Fascinations

Fascination means 'to bewitch and hold spellbound', they are flower spells and charms.

If you put together the knowledge you have on magical properties within flowers, herbs and plants it is easy to put together a flower fascination. It doesn't need to be fancy, just putting together corresponding flowers and herbs with the same intent into a vase will do the trick. Put the vase somewhere that you will see it and visualize your intent each time you do.

Flower seeds can be added to medicine bags and charm bags then worn or kept with you.

Decorate a small besom or wreath with dried or fresh flowers with a particular intent in mind or to celebrate a Sabbat or honour a specific deity.

Keeping a dried poppy head in your purse for prosperity, tying a bunch of sage over the front door for protection, putting herbs in a sachet to keep in the car for safety and protection – all of these are simple flower fascinations.

Types of Garden

You can also plant up your garden with a theme. You could dedicate the whole garden or a section of it to a particular deity and fill it with plants that honour and correspond to them. You could make your garden or an area of it into a garden for the Fae, the ideas are limitless really. I have seen herbs planted in a spiral to honour the Goddess, herbs and bedding plants laid out in the shape of a pentacle. A garden can be laid out in four sections to honour the four elements, each section having been planted with corresponding flowers and shrubs.

What about planting a planetary garden? You could choose plants that correspond to each of the planets, so for sun you might plant sunflowers, marigolds and rosemary. For the moon you might plant jasmine, pumpkins or gardenia. Mercury might be fennel, lavender and dill. Mars could be snapdragons, radish and holly. Jupiter might be meadowsweet, sage and honeysuckle. Venus could be violets, foxgloves and primroses and Saturn could be ivy, pansies and mimosa.

Faery gardens are very popular to create and can be very rewarding. You can create separate sections of the garden to attract different types of Fae, for instance a shady, earthy area for the gnomes and brownies. Generally the Fae like water, shiny things and pretty, scented flowers. You could also place a few crystals in amongst the plants for them too.

Protection Plants

As most gardens are in the boundaries of your home, protection is quite a feature in the magical plant world. In the summer months I have a large trough at the front of my home filled with red geraniums as a protection ward. Ivy is also good for protection as are marigolds. These can be planted along the edge of your boundary or put in pots.

Meditation

I find meditation extremely important not just for my own inner peace, to relax and release stress but it is also a good way of connecting with the divine and getting answers to queries or insight into situations that you may have.

Try to meditate at least for a few minutes each day, I like to spend 10 minutes at the end of the day just to calm and centre myself and connect with my spirit guides, my totem or my patron deity.

These are some of my meditations I would like to share with you:

Spring Meditation

Make yourself comfortable. Take three deep breaths... in and out...

As your reality dissipates you find yourself standing on a muddy track, to your left are open fields, and to your right is the edge of a large forest. The sun is just starting to peep over the horizon.

The weather is cold and the air is crisp, but you are warm as you are wrapped up well. As you take a deep breath in you can feel the sharp air, cleansing and refreshing.

You start to walk along the path; the earth is hard and crisp as you make your way.

You can hear a noise, and you realise it is the bleating of sheep. As you turn round a bend in the track you see a whole field full of sheep and you notice that there are lots of lambs too, some are dashing about the field, others are snuggled up to their mothers. You stop and lean on the fence at the edge of the field and watch them for a moment. This is new life, new beginnings. Some of the sheep make their way to the fence where you are standing; you can feel their warmth and listen to them as they bleat to you.

Then you move on, continuing along the track. The sun has climbed up over the horizon now and its rays of light shine across the fields.

As you look across the fields you see movement, just catching a glimpse of something... you stop and watch closely... it moves again... it is a hare. She darts from one side of the field to the other, so graceful and beautiful. She is intuition and creativity. She leaps and bounds her way through life. A reminder to you that growth is assured if you are moving in balance with what is occurring in your life. If you move too fast or too slow an imbalance occurs and growth is stifled. Once she has disappeared from your view you move on.

As you walk you glance into the forest, there are still some last remnants of snow in the deeper parts of the woods, but you notice something else that is white, smaller and more delicate just on the edge, you bend down to get a closer look and realise it is a snowdrop that has pushed its way up through the foliage and the snow. The first sign that Mother Nature is awakening.

You straighten up and continue along the path... when... crack!... you jump... you look down to see what made the noise and find that you have stepped into a small puddle that had iced over, your foot cracked the thin layer of ice on top.

You can also hear the sounds of the wildlife in the forest, deep within the trees. The bird songs calling out to each other that the sun has awoken for the day. The small burrowing animals are starting to awake from their deep winter slumber.

The sun is now well on its way up into the sky and its light casts streaks upon the fields and glints upon the wet trees and foliage of the woods. But something catches your eye just inside the edge of the woods, a sparkle, and a flash of light. You make your way over to see what it is. As you look down into the under-growth you see a small metal pot laying on its side, you turn it over and look inside. There, in the shadow of the pot, is a gift for you. You put your hand down and pick it up. This item is special to you; it is a sign of new beginnings, a new project perhaps, or a new direction? Take the item and put it in your pocket, it already means something to you or it will in the near future.

You stand now and slowly turn around in a circle taking in all the sights and sounds... the fields, the woods, the sun, and the wildlife. Capture this feeling, these memories, and take them with you.

When you are ready, slowly, breathing in and out deeply, come back to your reality.

Goddess Meditation

Settle and make yourself comfortable. Take several deep breathes in and out.

As your mundane world dissipates you find yourself standing on lush green grass in a valley between beautiful hills.

Breathe in the fresh cleansing air, feel it fill your body with love and light.

You turn and look all around you, in a full circle. As far as the eye can see there is lush green grass, interspersed with patches of pretty wild flowers. You notice at the base of one of the hills a glint of light, a sparkle – so you make your way towards it.

As you walk you can hear birds singing, it is a beautiful sound. You can smell the scent of the wild flowers on the breeze. You can feel the grass soft beneath your feet.

Your eyes catch a glimpse of the sparkle again, a flittering of light... or is it?

As you get closer you realise there is a large pool of water, it looks as if it comes in from the sea as there is a little sandy bay. When you reach it you realise just how magical and enchanted the whole place looks. The sun glinting on the water, little dots of light flashing and bouncing off the ripples of water. Are they dots of light, or are they Fae?

There is a large flat rock beside the shore so you seat yourself upon it and gaze out across the water, taking in the beautiful scenery and enjoying the peacefulness the place brings.

You watch as two swans come swimming into view, gliding effortlessly and beautifully across the bay.

Then you hear a voice, singing beautifully. You stand and turn to see a woman walking along the shore to meet you. She has amazing cascades of dark brown hair and wears the dress of an Arthurian court lady. At her feet bounds a small rabbit, keeping pace with her steps. She stops occasionally to look at piece of drift wood or a pretty shell.

As she reaches you she greets you and opens her arms for an embrace.

She then indicates for you to sit beside her on the rocks. She has an amazing presence… ethereal, beautiful, loving and caring but also one of strength and power. She talks with you, answers your questions, and shares her wisdom.

When you have finished talking she embraces you once more and tells you that should you seek her wisdom or company again you have only to return to this enchanted place, and that the Fae will guide you to her.

She turns and you watch her walk away until she seems to disappear amid a cloud of the same sparkling lights you saw on the water.

You take one last long look round, drinking in the sights and sounds so that you can remember this place.

You then make your way out of the bay and back onto the grass, spread out before you.

Taking three long breaths; the beautiful hills disappear and are replaced by your usual surroundings.

Spiral Meditation

Close your eyes and take three deep breathes in and out. Releasing all the stresses and worries as you breathe out and visualizing bright white cleansing light filling you as you breathe in.

As you open your eyes you realize you are in a green field, the sun is shining and there is a warm breeze.

You can hear the birds singing.

You look up and see a small group of trees at the edge of the field and notice that you are standing on a path that leads to them.

You decide to make your way along the path.

When you reach the trees you hesitate, there is a quiet stillness about it, but you take a deep breath and step forward.

The air is cooler and the trees form a roof above your head casting shadows.

The twigs and leaves crunch under foot.

As you walk a little further you realize you are approaching a clearing. A few steps further and you step into shafts of warm sunlight.

You are standing in a sacred space in the centre of the trees.

The grass is lush and green and the clearing is edged with sweet smelling flowers.

In the centre is a large grey stone, you walk towards it.

As you near it you see there are some markings on it. You look closer and see that a spiral has been carved into the stone.

You run your finger over the spiral, following it round and round. As you do so you feel a tingle running up your arm from the spiral. As you follow the spiral round with your hand a beautiful cleansing, energizing light pours into your body.

When you reach the end of the spiral you take a step back – you feel wonderful.

You realize the sun has moved across the sky and dusk is settling in.

You make your way back to the edge of the clearing, turning to look back over your shoulder at the beautiful sacred space.

Then you make your way back along the path, through the trees and out into the field.

You feel refreshed, regenerated and ready to deal with any new challenges.

Taking three long breaths, return to your reality.

Paradise Island Meditation

Ground and centre yourself, take three deep breaths in and out and release all your worries and stresses of the day.

You are in a small boat gently making its way to the shore of a beautiful island. It's just you and your boat, letting the waves take the boat ashore. The sky is clear blue; the sea is a shimmering aqua. The sun is warm and welcoming. There are no sounds but the lapping of the water on the side of the boat and, as you approach the shore, the sounds of the waves meeting the sand.

As your boat draws to a halt on the beach you step out onto gorgeous hot, soft white sand and your toes are enveloped by the warmth. You look up to see a forest of dark green luscious trees in front of you, so you make your way across the sand.

There is a gentle cooling breeze bringing the scent of the sea and the taste of salt to your lips.

You step into the canopy of trees where it is cool and refreshing. Lush greenery covers the floor and as you gaze upwards there is a dark green sky of leaves. The air is warm and moist.

You can hear the sound of running water, not the sea but something else, so you make your way through the trees following the sound.

You come to the other side of the forest. Just by the edge of the trees, there is a cliff of grey stone in front of you with a small waterfall running from the top and splashing down into a deep, dark blue pool of water. You sit down on a rock at the side of the pool and dip your feet in; the water is beautifully cool and refreshing. So refreshing, you decide to go further in. You slide from the rock into the water; it is so cool and cleansing. The water washes over you, cool on your skin. You gently swim to the other side of the pool and climb out – you feel radiant, energized and totally at peace.

You walk from the edge of the trees out into the sunlight and back onto the beach, it is the same beach you landed upon, but you are further down, so you slowly walk along the soft sand, allowing the sun to dry you as you walk, feeling its warm rays on you. Back to your little boat, you climb in and push the boat off, back into the sea and head for the sun, which is now setting on the horizon. You feel refreshed and rejuvenated.

Taking three long breaths, return to your reality.

Tintagel Meditation

Sit comfortably; take three deep breaths…in and out slowly.

Visualize all the stresses and worries of the day disappearing with each breath out.

As the real world disappears, you find yourself at the bottom of a steep street. As you look up in front of you, there is a tall hill with a steep winding stone staircase. The stairway is built of old, grey stone.

The hill is surrounded on three sides with the sea. Huge waves are crashing against the cliffs at the bottom. Seagulls are circling round, screeching and calling to each other. You can taste the salt in the air.

You walk towards the steps and start your climb upwards, taking each step slowly as the stairs are uneven and very narrow. With each step you relax a little more, feeling more peaceful in yourself.

The stairs wind steadily round and up, until you walk through a small stone archway at the top. This takes you out onto a flat area of grass where there are parts of grey stone walls, crumbled and abandoned. Lone rocks lie fallen; this was once a great and glorious castle… you have reached Tintagel Castle, once home to Arthur Pendragon.

The air is still, you can't hear a sound, not even the sea. It is so very peaceful, calm and quiet; broken only by the odd seagull as it swoops overhead.

You walk further onto the grass and turn to look out to your right. You can see the shoreline, the waves tumbling onto the sand and a large cave mouth... the home of Merlin the Sorcerer.

A warm breeze comes up from the sea; it winds itself around your legs, your body, your arms, and your face. You feel it clearing out all the cobwebs; blowing away all your worries, taking all your stresses with it.

The breeze brings with it faint voices... laughter, talking, the sound of a jester, horses braying and people clapping. You can't make it out at first until you realize it is echoes of the court that once was.

You can feel a tingle on your skin, but you are not sure what it is... until you realize it is the feeling of magic in the air. You can almost see the ghosts of Merlin's spells dancing and chasing around in the air. You can feel and taste the spark of ancient magic in the air all around you.

You stand for a moment, taking it all in.

Whilst you have been standing here, the moon has started to climb up into the sky, she is full and round and beautiful. You stand and gaze up at her. Breathe in her light until it fills your body with silvery essence.

You get a sense of love, of comfort and contentment, a feeling of having come home. Hold onto these feelings as you turn and make your way across the grass back to the archway.

You gradually make your way back down the stone stairway, with each step it brings you back to us, step by step, step by step. Down and around.

When you reach the ground you feel refreshed and renewed and full of ancient magic.

Taking three long breaths, return to your reality.

Autumn Melodies Meditation

Sit comfortably and start to relax as your world dissipates and is replaced...

You are standing outside a thatched cottage, the sky is a beautiful clear blue and the sun is shining, but the air is crisp and cool. It is a beautiful autumn morning. Laid out before you is a cottage garden, full of dahlias, chrysanthemums and geraniums. A gorgeous kaleidoscope of colours. Amongst all the flowers are vegetables and herbs; runner beans, courgettes, mint, rosemary and pumpkins.

It is so peaceful; you can hear the rustling of the trees, the leaves whispering to each other. You look up to see where their sound is coming from and realize that the entire cottage and garden are surrounded by a forest. There are tall trees of every sort, the light breeze moving the leaves. Shades of greens, orange and yellow are everywhere as the leaves have started to turn. You can also hear the buzzing of bees as they make the most of the last of the summer flowers.

Then you realize you can hear a bird calling, it's a wonderful, cheerful song. You stand and listen for a few moments and realize it is a blackbird. The sweet song of the blackbird, how wonderful – a blackbird can teach you the mystic secrets while in meditation. He can take you to a mystical place full of age-old knowledge and wisdom.

You walk further down the garden following his song, along the way you take note of all the bounty of vegetables that are growing in the garden. And also the old foliage of plants that have given their all during the summer to provide their bounty and are now lying dormant, ready to blend back into the Earth.

At the end of the garden is a gate leading into the forest, you see the blackbird sitting on the fence post, but for a fleeting moment. In a flurry of black feathers and yellow beak he is gone... left in his place is one single solitary glossy black feather. You pick it up and put it in your pocket.

You turn and stroll back down the garden and as you pass through the door to the cottage you realize you are back in your own home.

You absent mindedly put your hand in your pocket and realize you still have the feather...

Come back to your reality.

A Starry 'Knight' Meditation

Sit comfortably, breathing in and out slowly. As you breathe in visualize a brilliant white light cleansing your body. As you breathe out, visualize all your worries and stresses fading.

Your everyday surroundings start to dissipate...

You find yourself sitting on top of a lush green hill. The sky above you is a beautiful shade of dark indigo and is filled to bursting with sparkling stars.

The night is still and silent. You sit there gazing in wonder at the stars above, and the beautiful full round moon.

Suddenly you see a shooting star sweeping across the sky... then you realize it is heading your way... you close your eyes as it appears to reach you, but nothing happens so you open them again.

You find standing in front of you a knight in gleaming silver armour sitting astride a gorgeous white stallion.

You can't believe your eyes! He must have arrived on the shooting star. As you sit there in awe he leans down from his horse and offers you his hand.

As if in a dream you take his hand and he swings you up onto the back of his horse and tells you to hold on.

He turns the horse and leaps into the air... you feel the rush of wind in your hair.

The horse gallops up, up, up into the starry night sky. You feel exhilarated as the knight and his horse lead you upwards, when you are so high up that you can almost touch the stars themselves he levels out and slows to a canter.

The stars are so beautiful, as you pass by each one you feel each stress and worry that you carry in your heart and head diminishing ... one by one. Each star seems to be taking away your worries and replacing them with love.

Then you realize that the horse is starting to quicken its pace and that you are descending back down to the hilltop.

As you land the knight turns to face you and asks that you keep your heart and your head free from worry; that all will be taken care of – he asks that you trust in the Goddess to keep you safe.

In a blink he is gone – all you see is a shooting star heading upwards back into the starry night.

You feel amazing, light-hearted, hopeful and positive.

The hilltop and the starry sky begin to fade and are replaced by your own familiar surroundings.

Come back to your reality.

MOON

BOOKS

Moon Books invites you to begin or deepen your encounter with Paganism, in all its rich, creative, flourishing forms.